QUEEN VICTORIA'S Life in the SCOTTISH HIGHLANDS

depicted by her watercolour artists

Delia Millar

QUEEN VICTORIA'S

Life in the
SCOTTISH HIGHLANDS

depicted by her watercolour artists

Philip Wilson Publishers Limited

© Delia Millar 1985

First published by
Philip Wilson Publishers Limited
Russell Chambers, Covent Garden
London WC2E 8AA

Distributed in the USA by
Harper & Row, Publishers, Inc
10 East 53rd Street,
New York, NY 10022

ISBN 0 85667 194 0
Library of Congress Catalog Card Number 85—050361

Designed by Mary Osborne
Printed in Great Britain by
Acolortone Limited, Ipswich
and bound by Hunter and Foulis Limited, Edinburgh.

Contents

Abbreviations

Dearest Child: Dearest Child, 1858-61, ed R.Fulford (1964)

Dearest Mama: Dearest Mama, 1861-64, ed R.Fulford (1968)

Your Dear Letter: Your Dear Letter, 1865-71, ed R.Fulford (1971).
The three volumes edited by Roger Fulford contain a selection of the correspondence between Queen Victoria and her eldest daughter, the Crown Princess of Prussia.

Journal: Queen Victoria's Journal. This survives in the Royal Archives in the original form from 1832 to 1836 and in a reliable typescript copy up to the time of her marriage. From 1840 there remains only the imperfect copy made by her youngest daughter, Princess Beatrice. As her mother's executrix, she copied parts of the Journal and then destroyed the original.

Leaves: Leaves from the Journal of Our Life in the Highlands (1868). Some references are to the private edition published in 1865.

More Leaves: More Leaves from the Journal of a Life in the Highlands (1884). For an abridged version of *Leaves* and *More Leaves*, see *Queen Victoria's Highland Journals*, ed David Duff (1980).

RA: Royal Archive Number
RL: Royal Library Inventory Number

I have preserved all the seeming eccentricities of spelling and the copious underlinings in the manuscript sources I have quoted. The original Victorian spelling of Gaelic names has been kept in the titles of pictures and, naturally, in quotations. To simplify matters for the reader, the modern (Bartholomew and Ordnance Survey) spelling has been used elsewhere. This seemed to be the only possible compromise, although the result is inevitably inconsistent. Some of the alternative spellings are given in the index.

Preface

In the course of preparing a catalogue of the Victorian watercolours and drawings in the Royal Collection, research in the Royal Archives revealed a great many unpublished papers about the watercolourists who worked for Queen Victoria in Scotland. It was clear that there was more material than could be conveniently used in the catalogue, so it seemed sensible to attempt to devote a short independent book to them.

I am deeply indebted to Her Majesty the Queen for allowing me to publish material from the Royal Archives and to illustrate so many of the watercolours in the Royal Collection.

For this book I have also drawn freely on the letters and diaries of Lady Canning, James Giles and Carl Haag. For permission to quote from them, I am extremely grateful to the Earl of Harewood, Miss Mary Herdman and Mrs Priscilla Allison.

I should like to thank the former Librarian at Windsor Castle, Sir Robin Mackworth-Young, and his successor, Mr Oliver Everett, for facilitating my research; the Hon. Mrs Roberts and her team in the Print Room for their help; as well as Miss Jane Langton, the Registrar of the Royal Archives, and her colleagues Miss Elizabeth Cuthbert, Miss Frances Dimond and especially Mrs Geoffrey de Bellaigue, who translated for me the relevant passages from Haag's diaries. I am also grateful for help in various ways to, among others, Mr Alexander Booth, the Hon. Mrs Drummond, Mr and Mrs Stanley Finbow, Mrs Ian Fortey, Mr Christopher Hartley, Mr and Mrs Martin Leslie, Miss Theresa-Mary Morton, Mr Charles Noble, Mrs Edward Palmer, Miss Virginia Surtees, Mr Michael Warnes, Mrs Peter Wood-Smith and Miss Bridget Wright. The facilities of the London Library have been invaluable. My thanks are also due to my editor, Tim Ayers, and my designer, Mary Osborne, for all the trouble they have taken.

I have received much help from my family. The manuscript was read by Cynthia and partly typed by Lucy, while my husband, Oliver, gave me unstinting support.

'Every year my heart becomes more fixed in this dear Paradise, and so much more so now, that all has become my dearest Albert's own creation, own work, own building, own laying out, as at Osborne; and his great taste, and the impress of his dear hand, have been stamped everywhere.'
Leaves, 13 October 1856

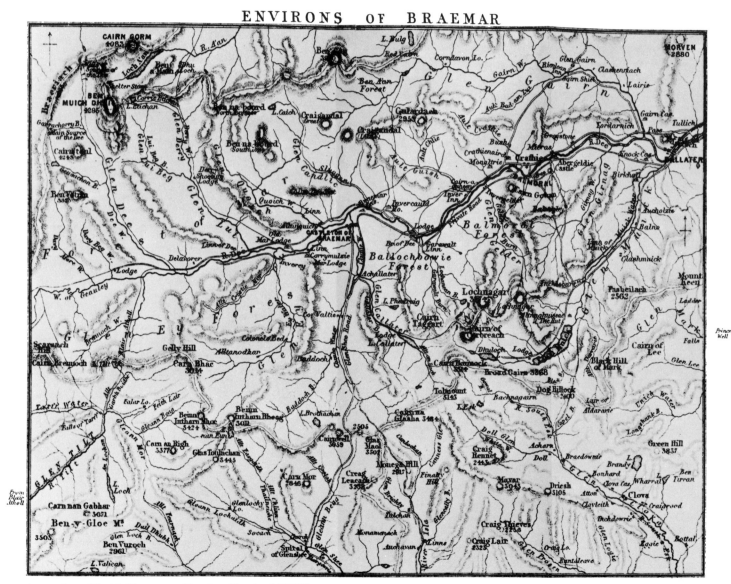

A map from Black's *Picturesque Tourist of Scotland* (1875)

Introduction

As soon as they acquired a house in Scotland, during 1848, Queen Victoria and Prince Albert set about collecting views of their favourite scenes in this 'truly Princely & romantic little Kingdom'.[1] Encouraged by her mother, as a girl, the Queen had compiled scrapbooks of watercolours and prints depicting places she visited. After her marriage to Prince Albert in 1840, he helped her to put these in order and they began to make 'Souvenir' or 'View Albums' of watercolours recording the journeys they made together. They spent most Sunday evenings and two evenings a week, whenever possible, arranging their growing collection of drawings. During the next twenty years, nine volumes were filled with over 600 watercolours, including more than 100 views of Scotland. They were bound in dark blue leather, 'with VR and the Crown upon them'.[2] Photographs and prints were arranged in other albums.

In November 1861, a month before the death of Prince Albert, the last volume was completed with a record of that summer's visit to Ireland. The Queen wanted to include two pages of drawings illustrating their expeditions in Scotland during the autumn; but the Prince did not wish it. After his death, the Queen decided that she would add them and 'finish for ever these most valuable and most precious books'.[3] She had relied on the Prince to arrange everything in the albums and dreaded the thought of having to complete them alone. Princess Alice helped her mother to fill the final pages of the ninth volume with pictures of the last expeditions. Any watercolours that the Queen acquired subsequently were either framed on her walls, or kept in portfolios and smaller albums. Her Souvenir Albums were associated solely with life with the Prince and she usually kept them near at hand, even when she was travelling.

By 1929 the original Souvenir Albums had probably become rather dilapidated. With the agreement of King George V and Queen Mary, Owen Morshead, the Librarian at Windsor Castle, decided to break up the old books and rebind the watercolours in a new set of very large red leather volumes. Most of the works from the original albums were included, as well as a great many watercolours which were then unsorted in the Royal Library at Windsor Castle. Carl Haag's studies for royal commissions, which had previously been in an album of their own, and Kenneth MacLeay's portraits of Highlanders, were also absorbed into the new series, as well as numbers of French, German and other drawings from separate books or portfolios. The new volumes were arranged on a topographical, rather than a chronological basis. The Scottish watercolours, which had been placed at intervals throughout the nine old albums, were now all mounted together in Volumes XII, XIII and XIV of the new set. The rearrangement totally destroyed Queen Victoria's original intentions and only a typescript list now records the earlier layout.

In many cases, the Librarian mounted type-written transcripts from Queen Victoria's Journal beside the drawings, relating to the ceremony or place shown. At the time of the rearrangement, Princess Beatrice was still in the process of copying out the greater part of Queen Victoria's Journal and, following her mother's orders, destroying the original diaries. Thus most of the Journals were inaccessible to the Librarian, who could not realise how fundamental the chronological arrangement had been to the Queen's purpose.

As well as the large Souvenir Albums, Queen Victoria made up four much smaller books of photographs and watercolours relating to Balmoral, covering the second half of the century. These have remained intact and their contents are therefore still mounted in chronological sequence. Edwin Landseer's drawings and Haag's watercolours were always intended to be displayed framed, although they were not hung at Balmoral in Queen Victoria's lifetime.

When she visited Balmoral for the first time in 1848, the Queen inserted into the pages of her Journal a little copy that she had made from a print of the castle. Topographically correct, it was the first of many views she was to collect of the house. A good likeness, whether in a portrait or a landscape, was of paramount importance to her. Certain artists achieved exactly what she wanted, but she was a hard task-mistress and liked to follow each detail of a work she had ordered. Miss Skerrett reminded Landseer: 'Don't you know (you have had practice too) that when a painter is at Court he is not as <u>free</u> as when he is at home'.[4]

The Queen disliked paying more for her pictures than was absolutely necessary, although an artist's bill was invariably settled at once; she had a horror of running up such debts as her uncle, George IV, had done. On the other hand, she would not agree to a specially reduced

2   *Queen Victoria* by Charles Brocky
Coloured chalks, 56·3 × 43 cm, RL 22047

3   *Prince Albert* by Charles Brocky
Coloured chalks, 56.3 × 43 cm, RL 22046

Drawn some months before the first royal
visit to Scotland: 'Albert and I were then
only twenty-three, young and happy'
(*Leaves*). The drawings were
commissioned after the Queen had seen a
drawing by Brocky of one of her Maids of
Honour. Landseer particularly admired
the way that Brocky drew eyes.

rate, but preferred to pay an artist the fair price. She tried to be kind
to her painters and thought she was understanding and considerate.
Nevertheless, Sir Henry Ponsonby could have been describing her
approach to her artists when he wrote, in 1871, of the financial dif-
ferences between the Queen and her grown-up children: 'they want to
do what they like not what the Q. likes, & want her to pay for doing
what they like, while she is ready to pay if they will do what she likes'.[5]

All was well if a painter was prepared to execute a picture for her
from the exact viewpoint she had chosen, on the scale she had stipulated and at a price which she considered fair. For some artists the
prospect of a royal commission overcame their qualms, but others could
not stand such pressure: we learn of one whose 'nerves are gone', the
'incessant Royal criticisms are more than he can bear'.[6] Many, in the
end, were glad never to work for the Queen again.

Both the Queen and Prince had been keen amateur artists since
childhood. The Queen's early drawing lessons with Richard Westall
developed her natural sense of observation. She made studies of
theatrical productions, portraits of her family and sketches of any

subject that caught her eye: a gipsy, a peasant in national costume, or a picturesque child. Before her first lesson with Edward Lear on 15 July 1846, however, she had scarcely attempted landscape. He 'sketched before me & teaches remarkably well',[7] she wrote in her Journal. On the second day, Lear expressed himself very pleased with her drawing and during the next three weeks she had twelve lessons at Osborne and Buckingham Palace. When, the following winter, the Queen sent Lear, who was in Rome, a vignette she had made after one of his sketches, he was delighted that she was persevering with her drawing. He felt that he had 'done little enough to deserve so gratifying a notice'[8] from her, but he had in fact fired the Queen with an enthusiasm and interest in landscape painting that was to give her continual pleasure for the next fifty years. Hundreds of her drawings and watercolours remain in the Royal Collection. Of varying quality, they complement at every stage the watercolours that her professional artists were painting for the Souvenir Albums.

When the lessons with Edward Lear came to an end, Lady Canning, one of the Queen's Ladies in Waiting, suggested that William Leighton Leitch might instruct her further. Lady Canning was his pupil and, in the meantime, she had been giving the Queen regular lessons herself. The work of Leitch was already familiar to the royal couple. The Duchess of Sutherland had shown them a portfolio of his Italian views and they had commissioned scenes of Rome and Venice from his sketches. The artist was also at Blair with the royal party in 1844.

The first session with Leitch took place at Osborne on 30 September 1846, when the Queen found him 'a very good simple man'.[9] By the end of the year, she was able to write with pride, as she put the finishing touches to a view of Osborne, that she had done it 'really, I must own, very nicely, considering that I only started sketching in July'.[10] The following month she told Lady Canning that she thought Leitch an excellent master, whom she recommended whenever she could. Her lessons with him were to continue for nearly twenty years and she drew as often as time allowed.

She was pleased when her Ladies in Waiting could draw with her. She was glad if they were able to play the piano or sing, but if they could draw or paint she was particularly delighted. Over the years the Ladies included a succession of talented amateurs, many of whom made sketches that were included in the albums: Caroline Gordon (5); Eleanor Stanley (colour plate IV on p35); Georgiana Liddell; Matilda Paget and Marie Mallet. Few of Lady Jocelyn's watercolours are in the Royal Collection, although she painted with the Queen at Ardverikie in 1847.

The most skilled artist was certainly Lady Canning (4). She was in Waiting at Blair and on four of the Queen's annual visits to Balmoral, in 1848, 1852, 1853 and 1855. On the second of these, she painted a number of watercolours for the albums (colour plate III on p35). When

4 *Charlotte, Viscountess Canning* by Carl Haag

Watercolour, 35·3 × 25·2 cm, RL 17283

A study for *Evening at Balmoral* (colour plate XVI on p107).

Lord Canning was made Governor-General of India in 1855, she resigned as Lady in Waiting. She made no more sketches for the Queen, but drew copiously while in India and wrote to the Queen about the problems of painting in that climate. She longed to return to England, 'home now seems so near', but died of fever just a few weeks before her husband's term of office ended. The news reached the Queen and Prince ten days before Prince Albert's own death and much distressed them both.

In the early years at Balmoral a professional watercolourist was invited up to Deeside each autumn. In 1849 Henry Fisk was there; in 1850 Landseer began his project for *Royal Sports on Hill and Loch*; in 1852 William Wyld spent several weeks; and the following year, Carl Haag's visit coincided with almost the whole period of the royal holiday. For the next six years no artist was at Balmoral during the residence, possibly because the Queen and Prince felt that Haag had captured the spirit of their life there so well, or perhaps because the Crimean War gave them more serious things to think about. In 1859 Egron Lundgren went north and George Fripp was at Balmoral in 1860. After the death of the Prince, when the Queen was trying to recapture memories of happier times, she summoned back Landseer, Leitch and Haag, whose names recur at intervals thereafter. A number of artists who had worked for the Queen and the Prince in the south also came to Balmoral in the later period, usually to carry out a specific project; like George Thomas or William Simpson, both of whom had

5   *Abergeldie Castle* by the Hon. Mrs Alexander Gordon

Black chalk heightened with white, signed and dated 8 October 1853, 23·6 × 34·3 cm, RL 22385

The lease of Abergeldie Castle was acquired for the Prince of Wales in 1849, but the house was used almost every autumn in the 1850s by the Duchess of Kent. Caroline Gordon made this drawing for the Duchess's scrapbook while in Waiting on her. As Caroline Herschel, in 1852 she had married the second son of the 4th Earl of Aberdeen, an Equerry to Prince Albert, who appears wearing a kilt on the right in colour plate XVI on p107.

been executing royal commissions since the Crimean War. Many watercolourists made one brief appearance at Balmoral and it is tempting to conjecture why they were not invited again. Sometimes an artist went abroad, like Lundgren or Colebrooke Stockdale, but others, like Fripp and perhaps Charles Landseer, seem not to have produced what was required. In almost every case it is interesting to see the painters away from their usual surroundings. Haag is more commonly known as an Orientalist; Lundgren as a painter of Indian scenes or the theatre; Bossoli in the Crimea and Wyld on the Continent. All appear in a different light at Balmoral.

The work of new artists, chosen by the Queen after the Prince's death, has less merit. The Queen thought that her husband had wonderful artistic knowledge and she had no confidence in her own judgement: 'How often he laughed at my want of artistic taste'. She had been used to 'never doing a thing, or buying a trifle, or arranging anything or moving my hand without asking his approval – almost to a torment to him, but I never was happy if I didn't know if he liked or approved any thing'.[11] Sir Henry Ponsonby, her Private Secretary, could even write to his wife in 1872: 'I don't think she cares for pictures and she abominates a gallery or an exhibition'.[12]

This may well have been true of the Queen in the 1870s, but her love of the Scottish scene certainly did not die with the Prince. From their formative years together, they had shared a romantic interest in Scottish history and tradition. They had been deeply influenced by the work of Sir Walter Scott. Already, reading *Rokeby* in 1836, the Queen had commented: 'Oh! Walter Scott is my beau ideal of a Poet; I do so admire him both in Poetry and Prose!'[13] During the Prince's last illness she read *Peveril of the Peak* aloud to him. For them and for their contemporaries Scott's work inevitably coloured their picture of Scotland.

It used to be claimed that the Highlands were 'repopularised by Scott and adopted as a play-thing by a foreign Queen';[14] but in fact the Highlands had been opened up before the Queen set foot in Scotland. Writing from Mull in 1840, Lord Cockburn described the extraordinary number of foreign travellers, mostly English, who 'fill every conveyance, and every inn, attracted by scenery, curiosity, superfluous time and wealth, and the fascination of Scott, while, attracted by grouse, the mansion-houses of half of our poor devils of Highland lairds are occupied by rich and titled Southrons. Even the students of Oxford and Cambridge come to remote villages of Scotland in autumn to study!'[15] This was partly brought about by the extremely effective and fast coach services and, later, by the arrival of the railroads. Lord Cockburn found the people 'mad' about railways: the country is 'an asylum of railway lunatics'. He read in a newspaper in 1846 of the supposed 'incredible advantages' of a Deeside railway line and expressed his thankfulness that at least he had seen that valley before it was 'breathed over by the angel of mechanical destruction'. The

Queen, in fact, never agreed to the Deeside line being continued west of Ballater. Although she enjoyed the convenience of railway travel, she would have sympathised with the old judge's hatred for a haste that compelled the traveller 'to be conveyed like parcels – speed alone considered, and seeing excluded'.[16]

No one felt more strongly than Queen Victoria that Balmoral should be a place for quiet and rest. 'The getting away from London, from drawing-rooms and levées, and to a great extent from state cares and state conferences –...the getting away from all these things to be simply a lady living with her husband and children in a Highland château must have been a new and delightful feeling'.[17] The Queen was proud of her 'independent life', a life that 'no other Queen has ever enjoyed', and she hoped – in vain as it proved – that Landseer would illustrate it for her. She lavished much care and thought on the formation of her collection of watercolours, which can be seen as complementary to her own *Leaves from the Journal of Our Life in the Highlands.*

Opposite

I   *Angus Mackay* by William Wyld

Watercolour, 35·5 × 25·5 cm

A watercolour apparently given to the Prince of Wales for his scrapbook by the artist during his stay at Balmoral in 1852. Mackay was piper to the Queen for ten years from 1843. He was a distinguished performer and composer, publishing a collection of pibrochs, as well as a volume of reels and strathspeys. He became mentally unbalanced in 1853 and, six years later, was drowned in the River Nith, Dumfriesshire, while escaping from an asylum.

Following page

II   *William Ross* by Kenneth MacLeay

Watercolour heightened with white, signed and dated 1866, 52·7 × 41 cm, RL 20712

Ross became the Queen's Piper in May 1854, in place of Mackay. He had served in the Black Watch for seventeen years and became Pipe-Major in 1853. He published a seminal *Collection of Pipe Music* containing nearly 400 tunes collected from Scottish and Irish pipers. Described by the Queen as 'a fine respectable looking man, with a very soldier-like bearing & good address', he is here shown on the East Terrace at Windsor Castle, playing pipes mounted with silver decorations, which are still in use. The jacket embellished with cairngorms also survives. Reproduced as the third plate in MacLeay's *Highlanders.*

I

Chapter One

The First Visits to Scotland
1842, 1844 and 1847

On 1 September 1842 Queen Victoria and Prince Albert landed at Granton Pier for their first glimpse of Scotland (7). They were to visit Edinburgh and eventually the Highlands, 'where no Sovereign of England has been, since the Union, & none perhaps before, excepting Charles II'.[1] More than thirty years later, when the Queen was visiting Glencoe, she felt, 'a sort of reverence in going over these scenes, in this most beautiful country, which I am proud to call my own, where there was such devoted loyalty to the family of my ancestors. For Stuart blood is in my veins & I am now, their representative & the people are as devoted & loyal to me, as they were to that unhappy Race'.[2]

In 1842 the Queen was prepared just to enjoy the beauties around her, 'travelling about, & seeing so much that is <u>totally</u> new'.[3] The Duke and Duchess of Buccleuch,[4] who were largely responsible for organising the royal tour, arranged that the Queen should see everything possible. Wherever they went, Prince Albert was reminded of Thuringia or Switzerland and the Queen, who had never been abroad, found the Highlands 'inexpressibly beautiful; such high Mountains, sometimes richly wooded, & at other times wild & barren'.[5] Everywhere they went, they were greeted by enormous and enthusiastic crowds, triumphal arches and decorations.

They stayed first with the Buccleuchs at Dalkeith and then moved on to visit other great houses.[6] At Taymouth, where they stayed with the Marquis of Breadalbane, there was a great crowd and it 'seemed

Chapter heading:
6 *Taymouth Castle: Presentation of Game to the Queen*, from a drawing by A. Maclure, in *Queen Victoria in Scotland* (1842).

like the reception in olden Feudal times, of the Sovereign by a Chief-tain' (8).[7] The clansmen were 'plaided and plumed in their tartan array'.[8] There were fireworks, bonfires and reels, and rooms in the castle had been newly furnished for the occasion. Predictably, one of the moments most enjoyed by the Queen was the quiet time spent in the picturesque dairy, drinking a glass of 'fine cold milk'.[9]

There were nine pipers, one and sometimes three of whom played at each meal. The Queen and Prince became quite accustomed to this habit and liked it. She wrote to her mother, the Duchess of Kent: 'We have heard nothing but Bagpipes since we have been in the <u>beautiful</u> Highlands, – & I am become so fond of it, – that <u>I</u> mean to have a <u>Piper</u>, who can if <u>you</u> like it, <u>pipe every night</u> at Frogmore'.[10] It is not known whether the offer was taken up by the Duchess, but the Queen did engage Angus Mackay, on Lord Breadalbane's recommendation, the following year (colour plate I on p17). Mackay's brother was piper to the Duke of Sussex, who was ardently attached to Scottish customs.[11]

7   *The Queen Landing at Granton Pier* by William Leitch

Watercolour heightened with white, 25 × 36 cm, RL 19577

The Royal Yacht is moored by the pier, on the right. Alice Sitwell, then living at Balmoral, wrote: 'All Scotland is in agitation with the Queen's visit, there are very few ladies left on Deeside, so many have rushed away to Edinbro'.

Sporting excursions were arranged for Prince Albert. He found the 'exertion and difficulty of stalking was immense', although in one day he shot nineteen roe-deer, three brace of grouse, several hares and a capercailzie, which were spread out in front of the house on his return (6). On the following day, wearing his velvet shooting jacket, shepherd-plaid trousers and a white hat, wading through bogs up to his knees, he shot a further nine brace of grouse.

The royal pair were young and energetic. On the day that they left Taymouth Castle ('this enchanting & Princely place'[12]), they had already walked to the dairy and planted two trees before driving to Loch Tay. They were rowed the sixteen-mile length of the loch to the strains of Gaelic boating songs. They landed at Achmore, lunched in a cottage, then drove through Glen Dochart, Glen Ogle and along Loch Earn to Comrie and Crieff, finally reaching Drummond Castle after seven o'clock. This was the pattern, in embryo, for many later trips.

8 *Taymouth Castle* by William Leitch

Watercolour heightened with white, 25·2 × 30 cm, RL 19659

Leitch's watercolour, made two years after the event, scarcely gives an impression of the excitement engendered by the royal visit.

Excellent stage management and planning enabled the Queen to travel by different methods with the least possible fatigue.

On their return south, Prince Albert wrote to his grandmother: 'Scotland has made a highly favourable impression on us both. The country is really very beautiful, although severe & grand, perfect for sport of all kinds, the air remarkably pure and light in comparison with what we have here. The people are more natural, & marked by that honesty & simplicity which <u>always</u> distinguishes the inhabitants of mountainous countries, who are far from towns'.[13]

The Queen was also fully appreciative of the splendours of the countryside through which they passed. She would have echoed the views of one of her Maids of Honour, who wrote to a colleague: 'I longed for your pencil – what sketches you would have made! lakes, mountains, and trees, and then a Highlander appearing as if by magic in some beautiful wild path. I am quite enchanted with it all'.[14]

9   *The Royal George Arriving at Leith on 1 September 1842* by J. W. Carmichael

Sepia ink and wash heightened with white, 27·2 × 37·7 cm, RL 20272

The royal party travelled on the old Royal Yacht, in which was a comfortable royal suite, even containing a pianoforte. An Alderney cow was on board to provide fresh milk. When the *Royal George* reached Leith at one o'clock in the morning, a chain of beacons was lit across Scotland. The first, on Arthur's Seat, is seen in the background here. The journey was so rough and took so long that for the return trip a steamer was hired, which enabled a 'speedy & prosperous voyage home' to be accomplished in forty-eight hours.

After the visit a few drawings of Scotland were added to the first Souvenir Album, among them two by J.W. Carmichael showing the Royal Yacht in which the party had travelled north (9). The Duke of Buccleuch arranged for William Leitch to make a set of watercolours illustrating the tour to give to the Queen, but these were not carried out until the autumn of 1844 and for some reason they were not then presented to her. Forty-six years later the Duke's daughter-in-law sent the watercolours to the Queen. She was delighted with these pictures of scenes 'so intimately associated with the happy memories of the past, connected with that bright and cloudless period' of her life.[15] In 1842 she had few such souvenirs of the trip. It was only during the second visit to Scotland that it was arranged for artists to be on the spot to paint for the Queen.

'The second journey is a chapter of romance in the setting of real life. It is true that the two have become three, that there is a small personage carried on board the yacht, bowing with the intense gravity of a child, to add another feature to the journey... At Blair there was a little Arcadia for a few weeks... It is "the quiet, the liberty", which charms them above all'. It was so different from the 'royal progress full of shouting and gorgeous receptions' of 1842.[16] On 9 September 1844, only five weeks after the birth of Prince Alfred, the Queen and Prince Albert, accompanied by the excited little Princess Royal in a merino pelisse and straw bonnet, sailed in the new Royal Yacht, the *Victoria and Albert*, from Woolwich. They were on a visit to Blair Castle, lent to them by Lord and Lady Glenlyon. Lord Glenlyon was, two years later, to succeed his uncle as the 6th Duke of Athole.[17]

The long journey up the east coast was again made through rough seas, but as they went further north the weather improved. The royal party disembarked at Dundee. The coming of the railway was soon to lessen dramatically the hazards and fatigues of the journey to Scotland, but now the party travelled on by carriage. The Queen and Prince drove in a new travelling chariot, while the Princess followed with the Household, in three coaches. There was an escort of Scots Greys and the servants rumbled behind in a stage coach. The cortège wound its way through splendid countryside and under triumphal arches. Prince Albert was in ecstasies at the beauty of the landscape.

At Blair Castle the Glenlyons had moved into the factor's house so that their guests could stay in the castle. Rooms unused for years were hastily decorated and furnished. On their first morning the royal couple awoke to clear skies and hot sunshine. They determined to keep early hours and after breakfast, taken before nine o'clock, the Queen was soon out with the Prince for a 'delightful, beautiful, wild walk, of 2 hours'.[18] Lady Canning, who was in Waiting, records that the Prince decided to stay with the Queen all day and 'to shoot grouse the next day & to stalk on Saturday. So quiet has all the ground been kept that not a shot has been fired this year either at grouse or deer & not a grouse was to be had for the Queen's luncheon & Ld Glenlyon went out to get a few for dinner!'

Lady Canning's first reaction was that, although the Prince seemed delighted to be at Blair, the Queen 'is hardly strong enough to enjoy it thoroughly'.[19] The Queen's half-sister, Feodora, Princess of Hohenlohe-Langenburg, had lamented that in Germany it was considered necessary to spend six weeks indoors after a confinement and she envied her sister: Queen Victoria was walking eleven days after the birth of Prince Alfred. She was annoyed to find the walks at Blair rather long and steep, but she was able to explore most of the surrounding country by using her rolling chair, her pony phaeton and a specially trained Scottish pony (10). Lady Canning fought a losing battle with their host to avoid exhausting the Queen by long expeditions, but she daily gained strength and in the end was sorry to leave.

Lady Canning was hard at work painting, 'for the Queen wants views done for her in every direction'(11). She was out of practice and spent a depressing day trying in vain to paint the Falls of Fender. She

10 *Sandy McAra with Arghait Bhean* by Charles Landseer

Watercolour heightened with white, 17 × 25 cm, RL 20775

Lord Glenlyon's servant is leading the pony, trained for the Queen's use and later given to her. McAra wears the grey cloth jacket and waistcoat, kilt and Highland bonnet, 'the same that they all wear here', which the Queen later instituted as uniform for her retainers at Balmoral. When Lord Glenlyon, recently recovered from blindness, insisted on leading the pony, the Queen was in 'such a state' that she constantly had to get off 'to conceal her terror'.

found the subject too difficult and felt that she had 'made a sad mess of it'. On one occasion, she set off on a pony followed on foot by a cockney groom. She outdistanced him and told him to follow at leisure, but he mistook her route and never caught up. Stopping to sketch, Lady Canning accidentally let go of her pony's bridle. Frightened by some other horses in a field, he trotted off and finally took to his heels, alarmed by the rattle of her bag of pencils and paintboxes on his back. She had to chase him for half an hour before he threw off the bag and she could catch him, tie him safely to a tree and make a further sketch.

Throughout the visit to Blair Castle journalists were in constant attendance, according to *Punch*, eager to criticise and comment. Every movement made by the royal party was keenly watched. *The Times* reporter was said to be up at five in the morning, peeping through the park palings; the reporter from the *Morning Post* sat hidden in a bed of nettles to see the Queen emerge. The reporters of the *Morning Chronicle* and *Morning Herald* were apparently equally intrusive. The Queen made no mention of these inconveniences in her Journal and seems to have been serenely oblivious of them: 'After the constant trying publicity we are accustomed to, it is so pleasant & refreshing, to be able, amidst such beautiful surroundings, to enjoy such complete privacy & such a simple life.'[20]

Lady Canning knew how keen the reporters were to charge Prince Albert with cruelty in his sport; the next year, when a great *battue* was organised for him at Gotha, she realised the harm it would do him in the eyes of the press. At Blair, an unfortunate otter hunt was arranged when Lord Aberdeen brought over his pack of hounds from Haddo. There proved to be no otters in the area, so Lord John Scott carried one over in a box from Kelso. When it was released, the animal was hardly in a fit state to escape the hounds and the Queen, who had a cold, loyally watched the unpleasant scene that ensued from the back of her pony, clad in a macintosh and armed with an umbrella. *Punch* piously said that it could not believe these proceedings and the reporter on the *Herald* objected to the Prince's lack of sportsmanship.

Lady Canning was justifiably critical when he shot a half-tame stag from the dining-room window. The little Princess Royal wept bitterly. Her life-long dislike of blood sports may have stemmed from this moment. The scene made the Queen 'shake and be very uncomfortable', although she was unable to resist watching a similar performance the following day. The dead beast was brought round to the door on the back of a pony for the Queen to look at, the first of many such 'showings'. The Queen bravely commented that it was a picturesque sight and wished she could have sketched it. The Prince was not a good shot and he was constantly unlucky with his sport. The wind, the weather and trespassing walkers all contributed to his ill fortune. *Punch* reported: 'The birds were shy, but we suspect the "shyness" was on the part of the Prince's sportsmanship'.[21] He also went grouse-shooting and

trout-fishing, but the largest fish fell back into the water. From one day's deer-stalking, he brought back only a hare.

On 19 September, Lord Breadalbane came over to Blair for two nights from Taymouth Castle. He was included in the party that set out two days later up Glen Tilt. It was 'a long day indeed, but one which I shall not easily forget', wrote the Queen. They did not get back until nearly eight o'clock at night. The Queen rode Lord Glenlyon's grey pony, wearing a long shepherd-plaid apron instead of a riding habit. Piles of cloaks and a great luncheon box were packed on moor ponies. The procession wound up the hillside by a zigzag path, with the old keeper leading the way and Highlanders bringing up the rear with the dogs. Lady Canning described it as 'just like a Highland sketch of Landseer's. The Queen too wished that 'we could have had Landseer with us to sketch our party. If I had only had the time to do so'.[22] This potential subject for a picture, however, was not to be

11 *Glen Tilt, Looking towards the Forest from Forest Lodge* by Viscountess Canning

Watercolour heightened with white, 18 × 27 cm, RL 19516

The glen had been cleared in 1784 by the 4th Duke of Atholl, in order to make a deer forest. By the 1840s it was one of the most extensive and best stocked in the country.

12   *Glen Tilt* by William Leitch

Watercolour, dated 3 October 1844.
25 × 35·5 cm, RL 19664

The Queen called Glen Tilt 'our favourite
spot', with the river 'gushing and winding
over stones and slates, and the hills and
mountains skirted at the bottom with
beautiful trees, the whole lit up by the
sun'.

realised in paint for another nine years, when another artist, on another hillside, would see the possibilities of such a scheme.

By 1844 Edwin Landseer had been working intermittently for the
Queen for eight years, producing a series of brilliant portraits both of
her family and of her animals. In 1843 he had shown her a book of
'exquisite' Highland sketches, which had especially appealed to her;
she felt that they could now 'judge how true are the presentations of
the scenes & scenery there'.[23] At Blair she presumably saw Landseer's
early masterpiece *Death of the Stag in Glen Tilt* (101).

After hearing the Queen talk of Landseer, it was scarcely surprising
that Lord Breadalbane should have arranged for Charles Landseer, who
was on a visit to Taymouth with his famous brother, to go to Blair the
following week to make sketches for her.[24] Edwin was in good heart ('I
am much bolder, my appetite jolly – the weather fine'), but he was not
prepared to abandon his plan to visit the Duke and Duchess of Bedford

13 *Blair Castle* by Charles Landseer

Watercolour with bodycolour, signed and dated 1844, 25·5 × 36·2 cm, RL 19542

Lord Glenlyon's Athole Highlanders formed the royal bodyguard during the Queen's visit to the castle, as they had done at Taymouth in 1842. Lady Canning described how it consisted of about 150 or 200 volunteers, who 'do their exercise beautifully and are in full Highland dress and armed with Lochaber axes, claymores & dirks & pistols'. She did not think 'young gentlemen in England wd like particularly to volunteer to be on guard for three days together in a tent at the door…they declare it is a delightful life & they never were so happy'.

at Doune. His brother proved a poor substitute and Edwin found him 'very near jibbing' at the prospect of going.

On Charles's arrival on 26 September, he was met by Lady Canning. He had just missed the picturesque guard-mounting, so he was told to sketch the house and a number of figures in front of it; but he was not at all pleased with the subject and 'fidgetted about a great while doing nothing'. Charles Landseer had an opportunity to sketch the guard-mounting three days later, as he stayed on for a week after the royal party had left (13).

Edwin was most anxious to hear how his brother was getting on. Their circumstances were so different; each season Edwin moved from the shooting-box of one illustrious owner to another, before 'toddling' south when he had 'indulged sufficiently in Idleness'. He knew that Charles was unused to living in 'the class of society he finds here' and hoped that the commission to paint for the Queen might be of use to him, as well as giving pleasure to the Landseer family at home. He was delighted when he heard that Charles had been presented and 'made a good hit in pleasing the Q. and PA'. He anxiously awaited his brother's return, hoping that he was 'usefully, profitably and agreeably occupied'. Charles rejoined his brother at Doune on 8 October.

Perhaps the visit was not wholly successful, although he had painted four watercolours, for which he was paid twenty-five guineas. When the brothers met, Edwin was certainly much distressed that his ill-mannered brother had never written to thank Lord Breadalbane, as he had promised; Edwin had assured his host that his brother had done so. Charles Landseer never received another royal commission.

14 *Charles Landseer* by Solomon Alexander Hart

Pen and ink, dated October 184…, 10·8 × 9·5 cm. Reproduced by kind permission of the Trustees of the British Museum

Charles Landseer was described by John Constable as 'a common man', and by Lady Eastlake as having the same shrewd look as his brother, but less powerful.

About an hour after Charles Landseer's arrival at Blair Castle on 26 September, Lady Canning received a note from the painter William Leitch, who had been awaiting orders at Bridge of Tilt for the last twenty-four hours. He had announced his arrival by a card, which she had never received. Leitch was established among the aristocracy as a drawing-master and had made a series of views of Drumlanrig, while teaching the Duchess of Buccleuch the previous year. He was now about to carry out the Duke of Buccleuch's commission to illustrate the Queen's first visit to Scotland. He was to move on, in October, from Blair to Loch Tay, Taymouth Castle and Dupplin to make the necessary studies.

Leitch apparently came to Blair on Lady Canning's recommendation. On his arrival at the castle she showed him round, with the Maid of Honour, indicating subjects to draw. They walked for two hours, as fast as they could, and came home 'tired to death'. Leitch was delighted with his orders and said he would make a great number of pretty drawings from the subjects he had been shown. He did indeed make exactly the sort of local views that the Queen wanted for her Souvenir Albums (12, 16). Unfortunately his name is not mentioned in the Queen's Journal and he disappears from the scene to return two years later, when he began to give the Queen painting lessons. Nevertheless, six of his watercolours and six of Lady Canning's were arranged in the album, with those of Charles Landseer, when the Queen returned to Windsor on 5 October.[25] She wrote to her uncle, Leopold, King of the Belgians, that Blair 'possesses every enjoyment you can desire; shooting, fishing, beautiful scenery, – great liberty & retirement,

15   *Billy Duff* by Charles Landseer

Watercolour heightened with white,
25·2 × 17·6 cm, RL 20774

Lady Canning wrote of Billy Duff, who had been Lord Glenlyon's henchman at the Eglinton Tournament, as 'a savage picturesque keeper with a long black beard who was kept prisoner all night in the tent for having attempted to pass the sentries without the parole for the 3rd time'. As punishment, he had a breakfast of bread and water and was not allowed to carry the standard at the guard mounting. 'This playing soldiers is thoroughly enjoyed by officers & men'.

Duff was an original character, whose skills included tying salmon flies, knitting elaborately patterned socks, singing and playing the violin; see plate 92.

16   *Blair Castle, in the 'Den'* by William Leitch

Watercolour heightened with white, dated 30 September 1844, 25·7 × 36 cm, RL 19654

Opposite, above

17   *Iona* by Eduard Hildebrandt

Watercolour, signed and dated 1848,
17·4 × 24·7 cm, RL 13665

The Queen sketched from the Royal
Yacht (seen on the right), while Prince
Albert and the Prince of Leiningen
landed to visit the ruined monasteries.
One of a group of drawings commissioned
by the Queen at Windsor in January
1848, when Hildebrandt showed her
the sketches he had been making for the
King of Prussia.

Opposite, below

18   *Fingal's Cave* by William Leitch

Watercolour with bodycolour,
13·7 × 23·3 cm, RL 19679

'It was the first time the British standard,
with a Queen of Great Britain and her
husband and children, had ever entered
Fingal's Cave, and the men gave three
cheers, which sounded very impressive
there' (Journal).

– & delicious air. In short I am wretched to leave it & we long to
return to the dear <u>Highlands</u> wh. I feel I <u>love</u>, – I fear <u>more</u> than
matter-of-fact <u>un</u>-poetical England'.[26]

Three years passed, Osborne House was acquired and rebuilt, Coburg
and the Prince's birthplace were visited, and another little Princess was
born, before Queen Victoria returned to Scotland. Then, with Prince
Albert and their two eldest children, she left Osborne in the Royal
Yacht on 11 August 1847 and sailed up the west coast. A tour of the
Western Isles followed, giving the Queen an opportunity to see more
of her kingdom on one trip than ever before (17, 18).

The ten-day voyage was followed by a month's holiday at Ardverikie
in Inverness-shire, a shooting-box lent them by the Marquis of Abercorn. This remote spot, several miles from the nearest village or house,
was to prove the peaceful haven the Queen desired. The Prince wrote
in delight to the Duchess of Kent that the newspaper reporters called it
an 'uncome-atable place',[27] because they were quartered on the other
side of Loch Laggan and one could only cross to Ardverikie by a
floating bridge, which belonged to the house (19).

Unfortunately, although the landscape was beautiful, the weather
was dreadful. Even the Queen, who never liked to be too hot, commented on the 'pure but decidedly cold air'.[28] She sketched with Lady
Jocelyn, her Lady in Waiting, whenever they were able to do so, but
afterwards they had to walk to warm themselves, although it was
August. Lady Canning, who was not in Waiting but on a private visit

19   *Ardverikie: Loch Laggan from a Road
above the House* by Queen Victoria

Watercolour, signed and dated September
1847, 20 × 26·3 cm, RL K 26 f22

'I have never seen so uncome-atable a
place. Coaches passing near it, there are
none; villages in its vicinity, there are
none; farm-houses within sight of it, there
are none; peat built hovels within
anything like a reasonable distance, there
are next to none. The Queen, it is said,
wants retirement; and certainly, in her
present quarters, she has got it'. It was so
difficult to find that anyone seeking 'the
enchanted castle of Ardverikie', would
probably be found years later 'a
mouldering skeleton, grasping an
"Anderson's Guide to the Highlands" in
one hand and an empty whiskey flask in
the other', having set out years before
'to have a look at the Hunting Quarters of
the Queen' (*Illustrated London News*,
4 September 1847).

20 *Sketch of Loch Laggan* by Sir Edwin Landseer

Coloured chalks, 24·6 × 36·3 cm, RL 14064

A study used by Landseer for part of the background in the oil painting of *Queen Victoria Sketching at Loch Laggan.* Landseer stayed frequently with the Abercorns at Ardverikie. One of the Marquis's sons, Lord Ernest Hamilton, wrote that Landseer 'learned all his deer-lore while staying with my father', and although he was a notoriously bad shot, expected all the best beats.

21   *Queen Victoria Sketching at Loch Laggan* by Sir Edwin Landseer

Oil on panel, 34·1 × 49·5 cm

Landseer began this picture in November 1847, and was apparently lent the 'plaid satin petticoat with a blue bodice and scarf' that the little Princess had worn on her father's birthday in August; unlike her brothers, she had no outdoor Highland costume at this date. The Prince's kilt seems to be unfinished, painted plain red, without a pattern.

in the same area, was afraid that the visit would not have pleased the Queen. It was reported to be the wettest autumn for nine years.

The Queen was nevertheless anxious to have more views of the local scenery for her Souvenir Albums. In December 1847, Lady Jocelyn gave her some of the sketches she had made, but Lady Canning's skills were missed. Invited to make a watercolour of the Isle of Arran, Lady Canning worked one up from a sketch made on a visit the previous year (22). She told her mother that she had been 'pottering over' a drawing for the Queen all morning, as she had done one watercolour that proved too large; she had fancied the album was gigantic. The Queen liked the first one and wished to keep it, but another had to be made for the album. Both remain in the Royal Collection. Leitch had been at Osborne, giving drawing lessons, until four days before the family set off on their tour. He did not apparently accompany the party, but seems to have followed their route later to make sketches of the places they had seen.

22 *The Isle of Arran: Brodick Bay Looking up Glen Rosa* by Viscountess Canning

Watercolour heightened with white, 25·4 × 35 cm, RL 20203

III *Old Balmoral from the Opposite Side of the River Dee* by Viscountess Canning

Watercolour, signed and dated (on the verso) 11 October 1852, 28·8 × 40·5 cm, RL 19465

Before leaving Balmoral in 1852, Lady Canning made a sketch from the flagstaff above Crathie Church (now in the collection of the Earl of Harewood). It showed the castle, the Iron Ballroom, the game larder and the temporary staff buildings. She worked it up into this watercolour, adding the Purchase Cairn, which had been erected on the last day of the Queen's visit (37 and colour plate VII on p53).

IV *View of Glen Muick* by the Hon. Eleanor Stanley

Watercolour, signed and dated 1854, 18·5 × 26·8 cm, RL 16904

While in Waiting as a Maid of Honour at Balmoral during October 1854, Miss Stanley described her attempts to paint Lochnagar: 'I am afraid I am very bad at mountains; I never have half the trouble with my buildings, and they always succeed'. The Queen helped with the foreground and showed her drawings by Lady Canning and Leitch in one of the Souvenir Albums, which she found 'a great help, really, and very pretty to look at besides'. Thirty years later the Queen commented that Miss Stanley's sketches had done 'more justice to the beauties of Deeside than any others she owned'.

V *Old Balmoral Castle in 1850* by
William Leitch

Watercolour heightened with bodycolour,
31·1 × 45·5 cm, RL 19645

A view from above Crathie, looking
south.

When the royal party had first reached Ardverikie, the Queen was 'out of spirits & I fear humour', but by the third week of her stay she was writing to her uncle: 'I love this place dearly & the quiet, simple & wild life we lead here particularly, – in spite of the abominable weather we have had... Really when one thinks of the very dull life, & particularly the life of constant self denial wh. my poor dear Albert leads, he deserves every amusement in the world, – & even about his amusements he is so accommodating that I am deeply touched by it; he is very fond of shooting but it is all with the greatest moderation'.[29] The Prince shot deer, grouse, ptarmigan, black cock, partridge and hares. The Queen, who felt that she had become quite a 'Sportswoman',[30] fished and walked extensively, up to eight miles a day with perfect ease. The little Princess Royal caught, all on her own, a small trout and the Prince of Wales carried home with great pride a partridge shot by his father. Their holiday was extended and on her return south the Queen wrote: 'I was quite miserable to leave those fine, wild mountains, that pure air, – & I had become quite attached to it & accustomed to our simple life there'.[31]

On 16 September Prince Albert left Ardverikie to visit Loch Ness and attend a ball at Inverness, intending to rejoin the Queen at Fort William on the following day. Nineteen miles from Ardverikie, he met Edwin Landseer on the Bridge of Tulloch. The artist was travelling from the Black Mount to Doune, but he proceeded to call at Ardverikie to see the Queen, who was giving lessons to the Prince of Wales. She was just completing pencil copies of the murals that Landseer had drawn on the walls of the dining-room and ante-room at Ardverikie during a previous visit. Lady Canning described these as 'beautiful sketches in charcoal & coloured chalk of several of the finest ideas of his pictures. They are very large & quite beautifully done'.[32]

The Queen must have discussed with Landseer an idea that had occurred to her soon after their arrival at Ardverikie, that he might paint a *ricordo* of their visit as a surprise Christmas present for the Prince.[33] The small oil painting *Queen Victoria Sketching at Loch Laggan* evolved (20, 21), showing her with sketching materials and the children in the Highland dress that they had worn for their father's birthday on 26 August.

As so often with Landseer, there was a struggle to get the picture finished in time. The Queen was so eager to have it for Christmas Eve that she was prepared to forego any likenesses, or even agree to the royal figures being entirely omitted. When she saw Landseer's ideas in November, she was delighted and anxious that, in order to keep the project a secret, the artist should come down to Windsor for sittings while the Prince was out shooting.[34] By 20 December the picture had still not arrived from the painter's studio. 'Her Majesty', wrote Miss Skerrett, 'has not the least doubt of the picture coming', but tactfully offered to have it collected to prevent any last-minute crisis.[35]

23 *Old Balmoral Castle from the East* by James Giles

Watercolour, signed and dated 1835, 25·4 × 34·9 cm
Reproduced by kind permission of the National Trust for Scotland

Painted in 1835 for Sir Robert Gordon, before the completion of his alterations to the original castle.

Chapter Two

The First Years at Balmoral, 1848-52

During the Queen's phenomenally wet holiday at Ardverikie, her physician, Sir James Clark, was receiving excellent reports of the weather on Deeside from his son, who was staying at Balmoral with Sir Robert Gordon, brother of Lord Aberdeen.

Balmoral had been owned by the Earls of Fife since the late eighteenth century, but had been let as a shooting estate to a series of tenants and to Sir Robert Gordon from 1830. As British Ambassador in Vienna, Sir Robert was frequently abroad, but in 1833 he made the deer forest of Glen Gelder by clearing the tenants, their sheep and cattle. A year later he began to modernise and improve the little shooting-box (23), where he lived with his sister Lady Alicia Gordon, enjoying frequent visits from Edwin Landseer (25). Lord Cockburn, who travelled all over Scotland as a circuit judge, wrote when he visited Deeside in 1841 that he did not recollect ever having seen any place that struck him more than Balmoral.[1] From 1842 the house was let for three years to Sir George Sitwell of Renishaw, one of the first among many Englishmen to be attracted to Scotland by the pleasures of sport and the novels of Scott.[2] His third daughter, Georgiana, a keen amateur artist, made a scrapbook of drawings of the house and neighbourhood at this date.

With the sudden death of Sir Robert Gordon at breakfast one morning in October 1847, the lease devolved on Lord Aberdeen. It has often been said that he pressed it upon the royal couple; but when he was asked for advice by George Anson, Prince Albert's secretary, he wrote: 'I have sent for a couple of Drawings of the place, which I have

Chapter heading:
24 *Stag and Hind* by Sir Edwin Landseer

RL 14057

A design for writing paper, which was made for the Queen and first used by her in September 1851.

25 *Shetland Pony with a Deer Hound* by Sir Edwin Landseer

Ink with bodycolour, dated 25 September 1837, 9·9 × 13·1 cm, RL 14053

A sketch made while Landseer was staying with Sir Robert Gordon at Balmoral, between visits to Doune and Haddo House. The drawing was acquired by Queen Victoria in 1874, at the sale after Landseer's death.

in the country, and have directed a slight plan to be made of the House and offices, with the dimensions of the rooms...To say the truth, if I had the honour of speaking to the Prince upon the subject, I should venture to take the liberty of saying that I thought the project of a permanent residence in Scotland at all, was a folly. But if this folly must positively be committed, there is nothing further to be said; and in this case, Balmoral certainly offers some recommendations. The place is beautiful itself, as well as the surrounding district. The valley of the Dee is a dry gravelly soil, and the air and water especially fine' (26, 27).[3] Sir James Clark's report on the efficacious climate of Deeside supported this.[4]

Lord Abercorn was also consulted by Anson. He wrote that Balmoral was about the size of Ardverikie and that everything was in excellent order: 'The scenery of that part of Dee side is reckoned vy fine, though for myself I prefer the remoteness and wildness of our Laggan country...I think the place is so situated as to admit of great privacy though certainly not so complete as at Laggan...In short I think if it is desired to have a residence in Scotland, that it wd be very difficult to find a place combining soil, climate, scenery, house and comparative civilization of roads &c, with excellent Deer and other shooting all readymade. The only objection I see is whether the calibre of the place is sufficiently great to entitle it to such distinction; that it might be made excellent for sporting purposes in the way I have mentioned, I have no doubt'.[5] By February 1848 the decision was taken to

Opposite, above
26 *Old Balmoral Castle from the South* by James Giles

Watercolour, 44·5 × 63·5 cm. Reproduced by kind permission of the National Trust for Scotland

Opposite, below
27 *Old Balmoral Castle from the North* by James Giles

Watercolour, signed and dated 1844, 44 × 64·2 cm, RL 22056

Both of these watercolours were painted for Sir Robert Gordon in 1844. When the possibility arose of the Queen and Prince acquiring the lease on the estate, in 1848, Lord Aberdeen showed them these views and probably also the one in plate 23. The view from the north was given to King George V and Queen Mary by the Marquis and Marchioness of Aberdeen and Temair in October 1921.

lease the Balmoral estate as Prince Albert's private property, where he would have the opportunity to enjoy on his own land the sport he loved; Dr Andrew Robertson, the factor on the estate, was in correspondence with Anson about the gardens.[6] An agreement to take over the furniture in the house was signed in May,[7] and it was arranged that Sir Robert's staff should be kept on by the Prince.[8]

The arrival of the royal party on 8 September 1848 created great excitement in the quiet countryside. Crowds of people collected in all the villages along the route from Aberdeen and there were triumphal arches and flags everywhere.[9] The Queen was delighted with Balmoral. She wrote to her uncle: 'This House is small but pretty, & tho' the Hills seen from the windows are not so fine, – the Scenery all around is the finest almost I have seen any where. It is very wild & solitary, & yet cheerful & beautifully wooded.'[10] A week later she wrote: 'You can walk for ever; I seldom walk less than 4 hours a day & when I come in I feel as if I want to go out again. And then the wildness, the solitariness of everything is so delightful, so refreshing; the people are so good & so simple – & uncivilised, tho' well educated'.[11]

Lady Canning, who was in Waiting, thought that Balmoral would be a great success. Although it was not very pretty near the house, she praised the beautiful views and the great variety of drives round about. The weather was tolerably good, although very cold, and everyone wore winter clothes. They were allowed to have fires lit all day, which was a luxury Lady Canning had not dared to hope for. She described it as a very small house, comfortable for a few people, but 'with eight at dinner every day, besides the 3 children & their governess, there are 60 servants'. She wondered what they all did, especially as 'housemaids were altogether forgotten & two had to be improvisé-d who had never played the part before'. Lady Canning found little time for letter-writing: 'I am always at work at bad drawings'. The Queen sketched with her, enjoying painting in surroundings where 'it was wonderful not seeing a human being, nor hearing a sound, excepting that of the wind, or the call of blackcock or grouse'.[12] Prince Albert went out to shoot ptarmigan, grouse and deer. He did not manage to shoot a stag until the end of the first week, although the deer came down to the gardens of the castle and, with the rabbits, frustrated any attempt to grow vegetables there.

The painter James Giles must have been introduced to the Queen in the course of this visit. He had begun his career painting snuff boxes in Aberdeen, moved south in 1823 to study in London, then travelled to Paris and Italy before returning to settle in Aberdeen in 1826. He made a number of friends and contacts among Scottish landowners, including Sir Robert Gordon and his brother. Between 1838 and 1855 he drew for Lord Aberdeen a series of eighty-five watercolours of Aberdeenshire castles. Giles also gave advice on houses and the layout of gardens. He had landscaped the grounds at Haddo House for the same

28 *Near the West Boundary of the Balmoral and Invercauld Forest* by James Giles

Watercolour, signed and dated 1849, 30·3 × 45 cm, RL 19618

A view in the Ballochbuie Forest, which adjoined the Balmoral estate and was owned by the Farquharsons of Invercauld. It was one of the last remaining Caledonian pine forests. Already by 1842, when G. and P. Anderson's *Guide to the Highlands and Islands of Scotland* was published, some of the old trees, sixty feet high and up to thirteen or fourteen feet in girth, were being felled. The Queen finally acquired (and saved) the forest in 1878, when Colonel Farquharson was planning to cut it down.

patron and advised Sir Robert to alter and extend Balmoral, rather than rebuild it. A number of the watercolours painted for Sir Robert before 1848, which were later in Queen Victoria's collection, probably passed to her with the contents of the house.

On 7 September 1848 James Giles was at hand to sketch the Queen being greeted by Lord Aberdeen on board the Royal Yacht.[13] The Earl then spent two nights at Balmoral from 26 September, when the Queen wrote that he was 'delighted at my love for the Highlands',[14] and Giles may well have been presented on this occasion. Two oil paintings of Balmoral and Lochnagar were commissioned from him as Christmas presents for Prince Albert and the Queen also ordered three watercolours. She liked one of the oil paintings so much that she made a copy of it herself.

Giles knew the neighbourhood very well. Apart from working for Sir Robert, he had painted, from 1844 onwards, a series of views of the adjoining Invercauld estate. He completed the Queen's three watercolours by 7 October and the oils by 9 December. In January and February 1849, he was hard at work on a commission for five more watercolours. He began them full of enthusiasm and determined to continue without interruption until they were finished. They took far longer than he had anticipated and turned out to be a chore, 'but so it always is, every artist knows with what rapidity & certainty he can sketch from nature but how difficult & tedious it is to repeat such a sketch, impossible I do believe, two hours on the spot makes at least two days work in the house'. Finally, he painstakingly arranged groups of deer and cattle in the foregrounds and by 8 February the watercolours were completed (28). They were duly placed in the Queen's current Souvenir

Album. In June 1849 Giles was again at work for his royal patrons, designing table linen, with suitably Scottish motives, to be made up by Messrs Hunt and Son of Dunfermline; it was later shown at the Great Exhibition of 1851 (29).

On 28 September 1848, when the time to leave Balmoral drew near, the Queen was in despair that her 'holidays' were at an end. It seemed unbearable to leave 'this <u>dear</u>, delightful place', where they had been so happy and 'so <u>quiet</u>, – <u>mentally</u>, so <u>active</u>, – <u>bodily</u>'.[15] There were only her own sketches, those of Lady Canning and, later, those of Giles to pore over on winter evenings, as she made up her albums and remembered the inscription hung over the road to Aberdeen: '<u>More beloved than ever, haste ye back to your home of heather</u>'.[16]

In August 1849, after her first visit to Ireland, the Queen returned to Balmoral. She was greeted by the Prince's jäger, Macdonald, in full Highland dress and Mackay playing the pipes. The castle and its surroundings seemed especially relaxing. The Queen wrote to her half-sister: 'We go on quietly, happily, & actively here, – the great event being the good or bad success of the Sport, – or the Expeditions one has made'.[17] Prince Albert was improving as a shot; on one day he killed three stags in two hours, as much as he had achieved in the whole of the previous season. 'The good, simple Highlanders are so pleased to see us again & always so friendly & amiable'.[18] Charles Greville, summoned to Deeside on duty, had to admit that, much as he disliked courts and everything about them, he was glad to have made the expedition. The royal family, he wrote, 'live there without any state whatever; they live not merely like private gentlefolks, but like very small gentlefolks, small house, small rooms, small establishment'. The Queen was 'running in and out of the house all day long, and often goes about alone, walks into the cottages, and sits down and chats with the old women'.[19]

A young artist named William Henry Fisk appeared briefly at Balmoral that year (30). The Prince may have seen his work in the south. He was perhaps among the 'numbers of the most talented Artists', whose work the Queen later felt would never have been known had it not been for the Prince.[20] Fisk was present one Sunday morning when the Queen came out of Crathie Church in pouring rain. With a Raleigh-like gesture, he spread his plaid upon the ground, so that the Queen and her suite could pass over it to their carriages. He painted four landscape watercolours for the Queen's Souvenir Albums. His visit may have been a joint project organised by the Prince and the *Illustrated London News*, in which the drawings were reproduced the following autumn.[21] Fisk became a lecturer and drawing master at University College School and a minor follower of the Pre-Raphaelites, but never reappeared at Balmoral.

On 27 September 1849 the royal party went south. The following day James Giles received a commission to paint three more views for

29 and title page   Design by James Giles for a tablecloth, from the *Art Journal Illustrated Catalogue of the Crystal Palace Exhibition* of 1851.

30 *Birkhall* by William Henry Fisk

Watercolour, signed and dated 1849,
47·5 × 27·8 cm, with curved top,
RL 19520

The house was acquired for the Prince of
Wales in 1848. During his minority it was
rented out. He himself first stayed there in
August 1862.

31 *Looking down the Valley of the Dee towards Abergeldie from the Moss House, halfway up Craig Gowan* by William Leitch

Watercolour heightened with bodycolour, 43·3 × 32 cm, RL 19649

One of a group of six watercolours, painted in the early 1850s for the Queen's Souvenir Albums, which show Leitch working on an unusually large scale and in a free style. The figures probably represent some of the royal children with their mother or a governess.

her; of the Dubh Loch, of Loch Muick and of the loch in the corrie of Lochnagar (colour plate VI on p53). He arrived at Balmoral on 1 October and had a miserable time in the hills making his studies. The weather was bitterly cold, with sleet and snow. The viewpoints chosen by the Queen were very steep, not easy to work from, and he lost a sketchbook. When he left Balmoral after four days, for the first time in his life without regret, he swore that he would never go there again unless things were on a different footing, as he had had 'horrid bad treatment' from the House Steward, François D'Albertançon. No sooner had Giles reached home, than he received orders from the Queen to make two more views of the castle, which must be completed before he painted the landscapes.

It was the beginning of November before he turned back to his studies of the lochs and worked them up into finished watercolours. At the end of the month, he took them to Haddo House to seek Lord Aberdeen's approval. Soon after they had been sent to Windsor, Giles received a letter from Lady Canning containing criticism from the Queen. 'So much for dictating to a professional man', he complained sadly, 'had I been left alone it would have been very different'. Clearly Giles was not by temperament an artist to whom the Queen could express her every wish, nor would he willingly allow her to oversee each stage of a drawing.

Unlike Giles, William Leitch was prepared to attempt exactly what the Queen asked. Most of his drawing instruction to the family was given at Osborne, but he was also at Balmoral at least once in the early 1850s, when he painted six large watercolours for the Souvenir Albums (31 and colour plate V on p36). Leitch was in Italy during 1854-55 and increasing attacks of migraine meant that his son, Richard Principal Leitch, was employed from 1857 to paint those views that the father was unable to undertake for the Queen.

Early in September 1850 Queen Victoria was back in Scotland and sent a message to Sir Edwin Landseer, in which she expressed a hope that he would come to Balmoral for a few days during his annual visit to the Highlands. A week later he arrived to see the castle for the first time under the royal regime. Landseer must have seemed to the Queen the perfect artist to depict her life in the new setting and when he left, to her great regret, after a visit of only ten days, she told the Duchess of Sutherland that he had 'made a beautiful Sketch and some very fine Studies for a Picture he is to paint for us illustrative of our life & pursuits in these <u>dear</u>, beautiful Highlands'.[22] The Queen's Journal that autumn contains many comments on the progress of Landseer's work for this picture, which became known as *Royal Sports on Hill and Loch*; the Queen referred to it as the *Boat Picture*. The idea for the subject had occurred to her two years previously, when she was first rowed up Loch Muick by her gillies: 'We found a fine large new boat, into which we got, and Macdonald, Duncan, Grant and Coutts, rowed...We had various scrambles in and out of the boat and along the shore, and saw three hawks and caught seventy trout. I wish an artist could have been there to sketch the scene; it was so picturesque – the boat, the net, and all those people in their kilts in the water and on the shore'.[23]

The expedition up the loch was repeated the day before Landseer's arrival and the Queen and Prince rode back to their little shiel, Allt-na-guibhsaich, on the newly made track along the shore, while the gillies rowed the boat beside them to the sound of the pipes. The Queen was reminded of the *Lady of the Lake* and quoted in her Journal:

> 'Ever, as on they bore, more loud
> And louder rung the pilbroch proud.
> At first the sound, by distance tame,
> Mellow'd along the waters came,
> And, lingering long by cape and bay,
> Wail'd every harsher note away'.[24]

On 17 September 1850, the day after his arrival, Landseer went up to the loch. 'The Lake was like a mirror', the Queen wrote, '& the extreme calmness, with the bright sunshine, hazy blue tints on the fine bold outline of hills coming down into our sweet Loch, quite enchanted Landseer. We landed at the usual landing place, where there was a haul of fish, & upwards of 20 trout were caught. Albert walked round & we got into the boat & picked up Landseer, who was sketching a little further up'.[25] The Queen was confident that Landseer would capture for her 'the beauty, poetry, and wildness of the scene'. She outlined in her Journal the subject that he was to paint for her of 'our turn out here'. 'It is to be thus: I, stepping out of the boat at Loch Muich, Albert, in his Highland dress, assisting me out, & I am looking at a stag which he is supposed to have just killed. Bertie is on the deer pony with McDonald (whom Landseer much admires) standing behind, with rifles & plaids on his shoulder. In the water, holding the boat, are several of the men in their kilts, – salmon are also lying on the ground. The picture is intended to represent me as meeting Albert, who has been stalking, whilst I have been fishing, & the whole is quite consonant with the truth'.[26]

On the second day of Landseer's visit he showed the Queen his 'slight scribble'. She thought his idea for the subject beautiful, but would express no opinion until Prince Albert had given his views; he was 'enchanted with it', so all was well. Each day the Queen went down to the gardener's cottage, where Landseer was staying, to watch his progress on large studies of the heads of her gillies (33, 34). She was herself attempting to draw portraits in chalk at this period, especially of local children, and so followed his progress with particular attention (35). The four studies of Macdonald, Grant, Coutts and Duncan are drawn in a mixed technique of pastel, chalk, stump and

white wax crayon. They have a waxed surface, which the artist prob- ably applied with candle grease to fix the drawings. They were carried out in a few days with great skill and are the only wholly satisfactory works to have come out of the project. After Landseer left Balmoral, Sir Charles Phipps wrote to assure him that the 'impressions' he had left behind had been most successful.[27] As always with Landseer the first sketches, spontaneously executed, bear the mark of genius; but delay spelt disaster and the delay in finishing the *Boat Picture* was to become a tragedy for both patron and painter.

In the following autumn Landseer spent two nights at Balmoral. He admired the Queen's drawings of stags' heads, touched them up for her, told her that they were excellently drawn and himself sketched, in ten minutes, the stuffed head of a stag. The Queen followed the progress of the *Boat Picture* with interest, but by the time Landseer visited Balmoral again, in the autumn of 1852, it was still incomplete. Lady Canning wrote tersely: 'Landseer was two days here & very pleasant, he had not a scrap of drawing to shew'. It was not easy to combine social life with painting. He was, as always, excellent company, delighting his listeners with after-dinner stories, told in his 'society drawl of a bygone gener- ation'.[28] In September 1853, when Sir Edwin was again at Balmoral

35 *Archie and Annie Macdonald* by Sir Edwin Landseer

Crayons, signed and dated 1851, 52·2 × 36·4 cm, RL 20776

Landseer began to teach the Queen to draw in chalks in March 1850. In December, she watched while he drew two of the children of John Macdonald. He almost completed the study in one session. In the following month, the children sat to the Queen while she made a copy of his picture. She did not pursue her efforts in this medium and later wrote sadly that she could never manage to draw well in chalks.

and again painting nothing, he was introduced to Carl Haag. Haag was proud to have met the famous Landseer, whom he considered the greatest animal painter of the century. By this time, Haag had begun, with intense excitement, to work for the Queen himself; Landseer returned to London and, although he visited Balmoral for a night in 1855, it was fourteen years before he painted there again.

36 *Royal Sports on Hill and Loch*

An engraving by W.H. Simmons after Sir
Edwin Landseer, 52·8 × 92 cm

Meanwhile the *Boat Picture* continued to haunt him. It was shown
in an incomplete state at the Royal Academy Exhibition of 1854,
when the reviewer in *The Athenaeum* praised the rabbit and deer 'as
wonderful as usual', while admitting that there were several flaws in
the drawing of the faces.[29] In the early stages of the picture, Winterhalter had tried to help Landseer with his portrait likenesses. In May
1865, Landseer was borrowing back the chalk heads of the gillies,
which he had given to the Queen, in an attempt to complete the
painting. By 1867, when the Queen asked him to touch up the faces
further, frequent alterations had utterly ruined the surface. 'He used to
scrape out with bits of glass, which were broken to a curved scimitar
shape, and the floor in front of this picture was frequently covered with
paint scrapings'.[30] The Queen was 'very kind and lenient about it', but
realised that it would never be the hoped-for masterpiece. Landseer felt
'jaded' by royal commands and suggestions, 'used up and crazy'. When
the painting was shown again, still unfinished, at the Royal Academy
of 1870, Landseer took one look at it and almost immediately left the
room with a shudder.[31] Perhaps it is fortunate for his reputation that,
after the Queen finally took possession of the picture, it spent many
years in store at Windsor. It was damaged by water and at last destroyed in the 1920s. The gillies' heads, the engraving of the picture
(36) and a small oil sketch, which the Queen persuaded Landseer to

37   *The Completion of the Cairn on Craig Gowan on 11 October 1852* by William Wyld

Watercolour heightened with bodycolour, signed and dated 12 October 1852, 22 × 35 cm, RL 19483

'One Cheer More' – the final stone laid by the Prince. Beside him stands the Queen in red plaid and green check skirt. Mackay plays the pipes and whisky is handed to the assembled crowd (see colour plate VII on p53).

give her as being 'valuable to her as a remembrance of happy times',[32] are the only records of the project.

In 1852 William Wyld was invited to Balmoral. His work may have been introduced to the royal couple by Louise, Queen of the Belgians; she apparently ordered a set of watercolours of Brussels for Queen Victoria from the artist.[33] There are also views of Manchester and Liverpool in the Royal Collection, commissioned and painted in 1852. While at Balmoral in that year, Wyld wrote a letter describing his visit: 'I am getting on very well with Her Majesty, who altho' a Queen is one of the most amiable women I ever spoke to, and so completely does she put you at your ease that I am no more embarrassed in talking to her than to you – I have now been here 12 days and see no chance of my getting away – I hardly expect I shall leave before the Court leaves, for my hands are full of work and she is wishing for something fresh every day – The young Princes & princesses are very nice children and were they <u>not</u> of the blood royal <u>any</u> mother might be justly proud of them – they are very well brought up & perfectly well behaved & they play about me like little kittens. "Mr Wyld this", "Mr Wyld that" – "Is it not <u>very</u> difficult – I wonder how you <u>can</u> do it so quickly I can't!" & &…The Country is magnificent & the weather is fine & I am literally worked off my legs, for wishing to give the Queen satisfaction. I do not spare myself – from 6 till 6, every day I am at it!'[34] A number of his sketches are in the Souvenir Albums and give an evocative picture of the old castle buildings, as well as the Deeside scenery (37, 55, 70 and colour plates VII, VIII on pp53,54).

Opposite, above
VI   *Lochnagar, the Lake in the Mountain* by James Giles

Watercolour heightened with white, signed, 30 × 44·8 cm, RL 19623

When the Queen saw this loch for the first time, on 25 September 1849, she described it as 'one of the wildest, grandest things imagineable'. Prince Albert compared the lake, which was about a thousand feet below the highest peak of the mountain, to the crater of Vesuvius.

Opposite, below
VII   *Placing the first Stone on the Cairn on Craig Gowan* by William Wyld

Watercolour heightened with bodycolour, signed, 22·8 × 35 cm, RL 19482

Wyld's series of watercolours, painted in the autumn of 1852, culminated in two scenes showing the building of the Purchase Cairn, in celebration of the acquisition of the Balmoral estates (37). Here the Queen is shown laying the first stone.

VI

VII

VIII *Old Balmoral Castle, the South Front in 1852* by William Wyld

Watercolour heightened with white, signed, 24·5 × 34·5 cm, RL 19495

The service wing built after 1848 is concealed by trees on the right; compare plates 26 and 38. A dressing-room for Prince Albert and three 'wooden' rooms for Princess Helena and her governess had recently been erected on the left, above and behind the conservatory.

IX *New Balmoral Castle, Design for the North-west Front* by James Giles

Watercolour, signed and dated 1853, 50·5 × 70 cm, RL 21524

'Scotch Baronial is the style adopted, but in a <u>modified</u> form' (*The Builder*, 13 January 1855).

Chapter Three

The Architecture and Interiors at Balmoral

I t was obvious on their first visit to Balmoral in 1848 that Sir Robert Gordon's shooting-box would not be large enough to serve as even the simplest holiday home for the rapidly increasing royal family. Each year another child was considered old enough to join the party that travelled north at the end of the London season. More servants were needed as well.

Sir Robert Gordon had employed the Aberdeen architect, John Smith, for his alterations to Balmoral. Prince Albert summoned the same architect, with his son William, and on 22 September 1848 they were already discussing improvements and additions.[1] New kitchens and offices were built before the next royal visit. Cottages, kennels and a venison larder followed. In July 1849 James Giles was asked to draw a realised view of the entrance front of the house, incorporating the architect's suggestions for large-scale alterations to the old castle (39). A slip or flap, in the Repton tradition, illustrates alternative designs for the right-hand half of the front. A window bay was to replace the entrance porch, which would be moved to the position of the existing conservatory. Alterations to the tower were also envisaged. Giles thought the design promised well, but rightly felt that it was 'doubtful whether it will ever be gone into'. A number of the features suggested by Smith were later incorporated into the design for the new castle.

In October 1849, just after leaving Balmoral, Giles received orders to paint two more views of the old exterior, presumably as a record of the house before alterations were undertaken (40). He seems to have worked up these new drawings at home and at Haddo, without returning to Balmoral to make them.

Chapter heading:
38   *Old Balmoral Castle*, from writing paper first used by the Queen in August 1849.

It was obviously uneconomic to make further alterations unless it was possible to buy the estate. Despite the high price asked by the trustees of the Earl of Fife, Prince Albert wrote on 10 November 1851 to Sir Charles Phipps, Keeper of the Privy Purse: 'I think we ought not to let Balmoral slip away from us, which would be likely to be the case if we don't conclude the purchase now, & that we can no longer live there without building & rendering the ultimate price thereby still higher, at the same time every pains ought to be taken to bring the price now asked, down'.[2] By the end of the month the estate of 17,400 acres had been acquired, although Prince Albert did not finally take possession of the property until the autumn of 1852.

In the meantime, other plans had been drawn up for alterations to the old house and, by May of that year, designs had been submitted by William Smith for a completely new house on a site with a better outlook, nearer the River Dee. By September, a definite decision to build afresh had been taken; the site was staked out and found to 'suit the ground extremely well'.[3] Building began the following spring

39 *Design for Alterations to Old Balmoral Castle* by James Giles

Watercolour, 43·5 × 63·5 cm, RL 21283

Giles began this drawing for William Smith on 28 July 1849. He completed it in nine days and was paid £20. Compare the existing house in plate 26 and the final new design in plate 41.

40 *Old Balmoral Castle from the North* by James Giles

Watercolour, signed and dated 1849, 26 × 42·5 cm, RL 19629

A view of the old castle with the service wing on the left, added after the lease had been acquired. Compare with plate 27.

The Prince took a detailed interest in all Smith's plans. He stipulated that the windows of the new house should be large. Smith therefore drew up two sets of designs. One was for the 'common sash' windows, which would give the most light; but the Prince preferred the other design, for mullion windows, which would be better 'in point of architectural effect'.[4] Great care was taken over which panes should open to admit fresh air. He commented adversely on the turrets in a design for the carriage porch, which he thought meaningless and so low in position that they looked like two extinguishers.[5] The Prince was determined that the outbuildings should be as plain and economically built as possible. He had a 'great horror of an influx of London improvements' and was 'afraid of getting out of the rough character of a Highland residence'.[6]

In the summer of 1853, James Giles was called in by William Smith to make two watercolours of the designs for the new castle as finally chosen by the Prince. These are so close in appearance to the completed house that they have always been taken to show it newly built (41 and colour plate IX on p54).[7] A model was also made. On their arrival at Balmoral in the autumn of 1853, the royal family walked

41   *New Balmoral Castle, Design for the South-east Front* by James Giles

Watercolour, signed and dated 1853, 50·5 × 70 cm, RL 21525

round to the new building, which the Queen thought promised to be 'very handsome'. The following day they examined it in detail, looked at the plans on the spot and decided that it would be 'charming'.[8] 'The new house', Prince Albert wrote to Baron Stockmar, 'is up one storey, and with its dressed granite, promises to present a noble appearance. The work is terribly hard, and for economy's sake the walls will have to be carried up several feet thick. The workmen, who have to be brought here from a distance, and to camp in wooden barracks, have already struck several times, which is now quite the fashion all over the country'.[9] The foundation stone was laid by the Queen on 28 September 1853. Although parts of the building were already up, the ceremony was delayed until her arrival, when it was celebrated with great rejoicing and a lavish consumption of whisky.

By the autumn of 1854 the Queen found the new house well advanced, very pretty and comfortable. Her apartments were built and the rooms for the royal children and the Ministers of State were roofed in. A new patent fire-proof method of construction had been used, with malleable iron beams. Eleanor Stanley, in Waiting at Balmoral, on seeing the new house thought it would be 'very nice, but not at all large for the number of people they will have to put up'.[10]

To record the various stages of the progress of the building, George Washington Wilson and his partner John Hay were commissioned by the Prince, in March 1854, to visit and photograph the castle at regular intervals.[11] They also made calotypes of the keepers and gillies. Dr Becker, the Prince's Librarian and a founder member of the Photographic Society, had also been making calotypes at Balmoral since 1852.

By the time of the visit in 1855, the royal apartments were ready for use, although the tower was still only half completed. A wooden passage connected the old and new houses, and the servants' quarters were still in the old building. The next year the Queen found the tower finished, as well as the new offices, and the old castle gone. 'The effect of the whole is very fine'.[12] Prince Albert wrote to the Prince of Wales, left behind on this occasion to continue his studies at Osborne: 'The way in which the buildings & grounds come out gives me much pleasure & surpasses in every particular my fondest expectations. The big tower looks very imposing & the difficult excavation in front of the house looks quite natural as if the ground had grown in that way'.[13] He was busy that autumn laying out the pleasure grounds. By the time they left Balmoral the Queen could write: 'Every year my heart becomes more fixed in this dear Paradise, and so much more so now, that <u>all</u> has become my dearest Albert's <u>own</u> creation, own work, own building, own laying out, as at <u>Osborne</u>; and his great taste, and the impress of his dear hand, have been stamped everywhere'.[14]

At the Great Exhibition, Prince Albert had seen the large prefabricated sheds designed in various styles by Edward T. Bellhouse and Company of the Eagle Foundry in Manchester to house emigrants who were leaving Scotland for Canada or Australia as a result of the Highland clearances. The Prince ordered one as a temporary ballroom for Balmoral (63). The design chosen, no. 1 Warehouse pattern, was a 'spacious structure of corrugated iron plates'. Although the factor had suggested that its erection should be delayed until after the royal residence, as the work would 'cause the deuce of a noise and bustle, while The Queen is here', it was in fact put up in three weeks and in use for the gillies' ball on 1 October 1851. Seen from a distance and 'tastefully painted', the hut had the appearance of 'a large cottage *ornée*, with two doors and eight windows, the ventilator resembling an ornamental chimney'.[15] The 'Iron Ballroom', as it was called, was used for that purpose until 1856. Later, when the old offices were swept away, it was resited near the new stables and game larders and is today in use as a carpenter's store.

Plans for a permanent ballroom were made after the estate was acquired. It was to be on a lower level than the rest of the house, in

42   *James Giles*

Photograph reproduced by kind permission of Miss Mary Herdman.

order to shut out the view of the offices from the dining-room windows and from the terrace on that side. By September 1855 the shell was complete and a year later the Queen opened it with a ball for the neighbours, to celebrate the anniversaries of the Battle of Alma and the engagement of the Princess Royal. The Queen thought it looked extremely pretty with wreaths of flowers suspended from the ceiling and stags' heads decorated with flowers on the walls. Lady Augusta Bruce, who came over to the dance in the Duchess of Kent's party from Abergeldie, described it as an immense Gothic hall with white-washed walls.[16] The decoration of the interior was eventually under-taken by Thomas Grieve, a theatrical designer, who had worked with Charles Kean on his productions at the Princess's Theatre and on command performances for the Queen at Windsor Castle. He went to Balmoral in September 1857 and superintended temporary decorations for that year's ball. His final designs were ready and approved by the Prince by June 1858. They were completed in time for the gillies' ball on 20 September. William Smith helped Grieve to carry out his ideas for the wooden columns, painted to simulate stone, which flanked the alcove at the side of the ballroom. Grieve had recently designed scenery for Kean's production of *Macbeth* and must have welcomed the opportunity to bring a flavour of ancient Scotland into the decoration. There were hanging targes, swords and spears draped in Royal Stewart tartan, stags' heads set on carved oval wreaths and Gothic woodwork in the alcove. A year after its completion, the room was the subject of two watercolours by Egron Lundgren, who had collaborated with Grieve on sets at the Princess's Theatre (colour plate XII on p72).

When the royal family first went to Balmoral, the interior of the castle was that of 'an old country house in bad repair, and totally unfit for royal personages', as the Earl of Malmesbury wrote in 1852. He found the rooms so small that he was obliged to write his dispatches on his bed and to keep his windows constantly open to get enough air. His private secretary was inconveniently lodged three miles from the castle. When the gentlemen played billiards each evening after dinner, the Queen and the Duchess of Kent had to keep getting up from their chairs 'to be out of the way of the cues'.[17] As the room was only 32 feet 6 inches by 17 feet, a full-size billiard-table must indeed have made play very constricted (43). In 1849 the Queen hung on the walls of the billiard-room and her sitting-room '11 prints after Landseer's finest paintings, mostly Highland scenes',[18] which she thought looked beautiful. It was the Prince's decision to hang engravings at Balmoral. The modern pictures they acquired were hung at Osborne, their other country home. Only in this century were the pictures relating to Bal-moral taken there from Osborne, Buckingham Palace or Windsor. In the Queen's sitting-room, in addition to the Landseer prints, there was a large engraving after Winterhalter's group of the royal family in 1846, a fire-screen made after Landseer's portrait of the greyhound, Eos, and

43 *Old Balmoral Castle, the Library and Billiard-room* by James Giles

Watercolour heightened with white, signed and dated 1855, 30 × 45 cm, RL 19472

Charles Greville wrote that the party retired after dinner 'to the only room there is besides the dining-room, which serves for billiards, library (hardly any books in it), and drawing-room'.

a number of stuffed stags' heads (colour plate X on p71). The furniture in the Queen's bedroom seems to have been mainly taken over with the house, but the pictures were her own choice (44). They included prints and watercolour copies by the Queen herself of works by James Giles and Philipp von Foltz (45). Foltz's original oil painting had been given to the Queen for her birthday in 1845 by her half-brother the Prince of Leiningen. It delighted her so much that she repeatedly asked him to find more paintings by this Munich artist for her to give to Prince Albert. She thanked him, in 1849, for sending her a view of the Rigi, and wrote of her 'adoration for Mountains...There is nothing like Mountains, Mountain Scenery & Mountaineers'.[19] To decorate the house, she also begged him to send the heads of any chamois or the teeth of any stags that he had shot.

Four watercolours of these interiors were commissioned from Giles in August 1855, as a record of their appearance before the old house was finally demolished (43-44, 46 and colour plate X on p71). Before leaving Scotland that year the Queen 'went over to the poor dear old

44 *Old Balmoral Castle, the Queen's Bedroom* by James Giles

Watercolour heightened with white, signed and dated 1855, 30·2 × 45 cm, RL 19473

In addition to prints of the Great Exhibition and engravings after Winterhalter portraits, the Queen hung her own watercolour copies here; see plate 45. The imitation rosewood furniture had belonged to Sir Robert Gordon.

45 *A Tyrolean Jäger* by Queen Victoria after Philipp von Foltz

Watercolour with bodycolour, 44 × 29·5 cm, RL K504

The Queen shared with her mother a passion for the picturesque qualities of Tyrolean scenery and costume. Helped by Prince Albert ('doing it much better than I can'), the Queen made this copy of a portrait of one of the Prince of Leiningen's jägers, painted on his estate near Hohenburg. She completed her copy on 19 March 1848 and decided that it had 'turned out quite a success'.

house, and to our rooms, which it was quite melancholy to see so deserted; and settled about things being brought over' to the apartments in the new castle.[20] In his diary Giles recorded that he worked on these interior views at Balmoral for twelve or thirteen hours a day over nearly three weeks in August and early September 1855. He then went to stay at Haddo House, where he continued to work on them for six or eight hours a day until they were completed. When he thankfully sent off the four finished drawings, he was told that the Queen was highly satisfied with them, but that they were too large for her albums. Giles had received no instructions as to size and therefore made the watercolours of the same dimensions as those he had painted for her previously. He was now instructed to have them photographed on a smaller scale and then to colour the prints. The wretched artist not unnaturally found this a very frustrating assignment. He toiled away all the autumn, complaining bitterly when the local photographer George Washington Wilson ('a stuffling slow coach'), kept him waiting for the last print. When the work was at last complete, he sent in his account for the eight drawings at the rate of three guineas a day, for 115 days work. This was what he charged less exalted clients for landscape gardening. He realised that the Queen would grudge so large a sum, but he was determined to be paid his due. He declared that he would much rather not work for royalty and that he had never made anything but a loss by it. He was, not surprisingly, never again asked to work for the Queen, but his large watercolours did find a place in the Souvenir Albums. The replicas were mounted in the series of albums containing photographs and sketches of Balmoral.

46 *Old Balmoral Castle, the Dining-room*
by James Giles

Watercolour, signed and dated 1855,
30 × 45 cm, RL 19471

Lady Canning was surprised at the
'enormous novelty' of luncheons at
Balmoral, where the Queen, the Prince,
the children, the ladies and gentlemen, as
well as the children's governess, all ate
together. The Queen and Prince often
returned to the dining-room after dinner
to take lessons in reels with the ladies.

The taste reflected in these interiors is
that of Sir Robert Gordon, rather than
that of the new owners; all the furniture
was taken over with the lease of the
house, as well as the twenty-two oil
paintings seen hanging in this room.

James Roberts was chosen to paint views of the interior of the new
castle. He was a drawing-master, who had come over to England from
Paris in the Revolution of 1848. He usually charged seven guineas for a
view of an interior and he was extensively employed in most of the
royal houses. Unlike Giles, he was quite prepared to colour up photographs. The Queen was more anxious to have a reliable record than
a work of art and, as photography was such a new and revolutionary
art form, painted photographs appealed to her as much as Giles's
carefully wrought watercolours. Twelve interior views of Balmoral were
commissioned from Roberts in 1857. Six of these survive in the Souvenir Albums (47-49 and colour plate XI on p71). Four more are known
from photographs of the originals (50), which were given to the Princess
Royal on her marriage. She was shown the whole series by her father
and selected for herself views of the library, her mother's sitting-room,
and her own bedroom and sitting-room. The Queen kept photographic
copies, coloured by William Corden from the original watercolours.

47 *New Balmoral Castle, the Dining-room* by James Roberts

Watercolour, signed and dated August 1857, 26 × 39 cm, RL 19475

Holland and Sons' bills include £58. 2s. for the 'best Turkey carpet'. The curtains are itemised as being of 'fine Tartan cachmere lined with merino and bound with plaited valence trimmed with a fringe'. Most of the furniture was oak.

The taste in furnishing in these 'cheerful and unpalace-like rooms'[21] shows a cosy mid-century approach with, naturally, a strong Scottish flavour. As at Osborne, the furnishings were largely supplied by Holland and Sons of Mount Street. Little of the material from the old house seems to have been incorporated; much of Sir Robert's furniture and the old pictures were sold in 1857.[22] Lady Augusta Bruce, on seeing the new rooms, found them very different from the old-fashioned interiors of the earlier house. 'The general woodwork is light coloured, maple and birch chiefly, with locks and hinges etc. silvered, and the effect is very good – besides there are beautiful things – Chandeliers of Parian; Highlanders, beautifully designed figures, holding the light, and which are placed in appropriate trophies – table ornaments in the same style, and loads of curiously devised and tasteful, as well as elaborately executed articles; the only want is a certain absence of harmony of the whole – in some matters such as the papering of the rooms – here and there fenders etc'.[23]

On her arrival at the new castle in September 1855 the Queen wrote: 'the house is quite charming; the rooms delightful; the furniture, paper, everything perfection'.[24] Perhaps only Lord Rosebery would have made the cynical remark, many years later, that he thought the drawing-room at Osborne was the ugliest room in the world – until he saw the drawing-room at Balmoral.[25] One person who was wholeheartedly delighted by the decoration of the new rooms was the Queen's German dresser, Frieda Arnold. She wrote a description of it to her family: 'Stuffed birds and rare kinds of stones found here are the ornaments in the corridors here, and of their kind they can well stand

48 *New Balmoral Castle, the Queen's Bedroom* by James Roberts

Watercolour heightened with white, signed and dated August 1857, 25·7 × 37·2 cm, RL 19478

The tablecloth is a Balmoral tartan fringed plaid. The furniture of maplewood was supplied by Holland and Sons, as was the Hunting Stewart Brussels carpet and the 'Thistle chintz' curtains and bed fittings.

comparison with the works of art that draw the eye in the corridors of Osborne and Windsor. Instead of the magnificent oil paintings there, here the walls are decorated with fine engravings in simple wooden frames. In the sitting-rooms are portraits of the Royal Family, and in the Salons hunting and animal pictures of all kinds. The furniture is of plain wood, tastefully made, and instead of the golden door-handles and bell-pulls, here they are of a kind of pewter with the letters V and A cast in them like this ⋈ , which has a pleasing effect. The upholstery of the furniture and likewise the curtains in the sitting-rooms are of glazed chintz, with a light grey background and the Scottish thistle in purple and green printed on it, which looks very good. In the salons this is poplin, with the Royal or Balmoral check, table-covers and carpets all of the same design. So everywhere one looks there is the most beautiful harmony, which gives one a very pleasant feeling; the wall-lights are silver antlers, guns or game-bags, and if one's pen needs dipping, one must look for ink in the back of a hound or a boar

49 *New Balmoral Castle, the Staircase* by James Roberts

Watercolour, signed and dated August 1857, 28·2 × 33·5 cm, RL 19474

The walls of the staircase and corridors were painted to imitate marble. The stags whose heads decorate the walls were all shot by the Prince. After his death, a memorandum from the Queen of 16 May 1862 ordered that the head of no stag shot by the Prince Consort should be removed, nor should any shot by other Princes be mounted on the walls.

– who could describe all these little things, which if they are well chosen enhance a castle so well'.[26]

Frieda Arnold, young and unsophisticated, could enjoy the simplicity of Balmoral after working among the splendours of Windsor or Buckingham Palace. She was glad to climb a plain wooden staircase again, but circumstances were different for the Queen's Ministers in Attendance, who had perforce to make the long and arduous journey to Deeside. The journey to Osborne was bad enough; Balmoral was a great deal worse. Lord Clarendon made his first visit to the Highlands on 30 August 1856, having previously 'always stopped with the nightingale south of the Tweed'.[27] He wrote sourly: 'Here everything is Scotch – the curtains, the carpets, the furniture are all of different plaids, and the thistles are in such abundance that they would rejoice the heart of a donkey if they happened to look like his favorite repast, which they don't. I am told that it is de rigueur to clothe myself in tweed directly...It is very cold here, and I believe my feet were frostbitten at dinner, for there was no fire at all there, and in the drawing-room there were two little sticks which hissed at the man who attempted to light them'.[28] On his next visit the following year Lord Clarendon complained that, although he had an excellent fire in his room, there was no heating in the drawing-room or dining-room, because it was August; 'The Queen seeming to have no more intention of a fire than

50   *New Balmoral Castle, the Library* by James Roberts

A photograph of one of the watercolours taken to Germany by the Princess Royal on her marriage.

The Queen and Prince normally took breakfast and lunch in this room and occasionally dined here alone. After the death of the Prince, the Queen used it for all her meals. Through the door at the back can be seen the staircase; the door on the left opens into the drawing-room. Holland and Sons' bills for the furniture in this room itemise the 'large handsome sofa', covered in button tufted claret morocco, with Clanwilliam and Sefton easy chairs to match; 140 yards of 'fine scarlet cloth book-falls with scalloped edges' was supplied for the library bookcases.

she would have in London a month ago'.[29] He described the Portuguese minister, Count Lavradio, who arrived at the castle in the middle of the night, having great difficulty getting in ('no drowned rat ever looked half so drowned as he') and carrying off with him 'poor notions of Highland climate'. The fireless drawing-room 'shrivelled him into nothing, and the Queen had the windows open while we were at dinner'.[30]

After the death of the Prince Consort, the Queen's life at Balmoral became infinitely simpler. Meals were usually taken in the library and after dinner she sat in the Prince's room upstairs with her daughters, sewing or knitting while a Lady in Waiting read aloud. The gentlemen played bowls or billiards or used the smoking-room, specially built in 1866. The Queen intensely disliked the habit of smoking and gave orders that the room should be closed and the lights put out at midnight, ostensibly so that the servants, who had to rise early in the morning, should not be kept up late.

51 *The Christening of Princess Victoria Eugenie of Battenberg* by Robert T. Pritchett

Watercolour, signed, 16·5 × 24 cm, RL 23189

Queen Victoria was delighted by the birth at Balmoral of the second child of Princess Beatrice, Princess Henry of Battenberg, 'the first time that there has been a birth in the Royal Family in Scotland since 1602'. The christening took place in the drawing-room on 23 November 1887. The lily font, the flowers and plants were brought from Windsor. Pritchett's watercolour shows the decoration of the room virtually unaltered since Roberts's view of twenty-six years earlier (see colour plate XI on p71). Pritchett had previously made drawings of Balmoral and Blair as illustrations to reviews of the Queen's *Leaves*, published in *Leisure Hour*, April and May 1868.

When he submitted the finished drawing, Pritchett asked that it should be shown to the Queen '*jour a gauche*', and waited anxiously to hear if it had 'passed muster'. As so often, there was criticism: the nurses on the right were too tall, the bottom-left corner must be filled up. Fortunately Pritchett could cope with such comments and altered his drawing.

Inevitably, the decoration was changed as little as possible from the original arrangements made by the Queen and the Prince together. On seeing Balmoral for the first time in 1884, Lady Dalhousie said that she never saw anything more uncomfortable or that she coveted less.[31] Henry Ponsonby, on duty at Balmoral, went to call on the Prince of Wales at Abergeldie in 1873 and was shown into a warm drawing-room, where the table was covered with books, photograph albums and magazines. He found it 'so different to this cold empty horror we shiver in here'. When the Duchess of Teck stayed at Balmoral in 1868, she described being shown by the Queen 'the little turret-room poor Albert used as a dressing-room & his bath-room, both left as tho' he were about to use them'.[32] Around the curved walls of the turret-room were framed twenty-two *cartes-de-visite* photographs of the beloved Prince.

Chapter Four

The Queen's Interest in Tartan
and the Highland Games

The visit of George IV to Edinburgh in 1822 excited tumultuous enthusiasm. One in every seven of Scotland's population is said to have been present to greet him. From the moment it was known that he was coming, everyone wanted to wear tartan in emulation of their Hanoverian monarch, who was to appear among them dressed, at enormous expense, in full Highland costume.[1] Messrs Wilson of Bannockburn had forty extra looms at work to meet the demand. Before this date, the only clan tartans with any real claim to authenticity were the Black Watch and those copied from portraits showing sitters wearing family tartans, like the Gordon or the Royal Stewart. Both the future George III, in a painting of 1746, and George IV, in David Wilkie's portrait of 1822, are seen in tartan approximating to the modern Royal Stewart. The Duke of Sussex was painted in Highland dress or uniform on a number of occasions.

From 1822 each clan chose or concocted a design and these were 'authenticated'. The short kilt or filibeg is said originally to have been evolved by an English Quaker factory owner near Inverness in the 1720s, who found the traditional belted plaid too cumbersome for his workers. At the beginning of the nineteenth century, it replaced the belted kilt as the uniform of the Highland regiments, causing amusement and interest on the Continent both during and after the Napoleonic Wars. Scottish dress and weapons had been proscribed after the '45 Rebellion and the act was only repealed in 1782. As a result, two generations of ordinary Highlanders had not been permitted to make their own kilts, plaids and hose, or wear their dirks and buckles. A

Chapter heading:
52 *Just Kilted,* a caricature from *Punch.*

large number of the poorer people therefore stayed in breeches after the repeal of the law. It was cheaper and many of the measuring sticks with which they contrived the patterns of their tartans had been lost in the intervening years.[2]

The new passion for tartan was an upper or middle-class enthusiasm, partly stimulated by the novels of Scott. 'As long as the Gaelic dress was worn', wrote Macaulay in the middle of the century, 'the Saxons had pronounced it hideous, ridiculous, nay, grossly indecent. Soon after it had been prohibited, they discovered that it was the most graceful drapery in Europe. The Gaelic monuments, the Gaelic usages, the Gaelic superstitions, the Gaelic verses, disdainfully neglected during many ages, began to attract the attention of the learned from the moment at which the peculiarities of the Gaelic race began to disappear'.[3]

It is entirely predictable that Queen Victoria should have been a passionate advocate of this historic costume. As a baby of six months, she was painted wearing a 'Scotch bonnet' decorated with feathers and a tartan ribbon (53). In 1834 she sent her half-sister a 'scotch' dress and the pattern of a new tartan that she was planning to wear.[4] In 1837 her mother sent the youngest Belgian prince three 'real Scotch bonnets' of green velvet with a tartan border, described by Princess Victoria as currently the height of fashion for little English boys of the first rank.[5] In 1842 Queen Louise wanted a Scotch satin dress with gold buttons and tassels for her daughter, explaining that because their father was so fond of the material her sons also wore Scotch dresses.[6] Queen Victoria frequently gave her younger foreign relations Highland costumes (54). One of her favourite cousins, Victoire, Duchess of Nemours, received a satin dress of Mackenzie plaid.

The Queen dressed her own children in tartan as soon as possible. The infant Prince of Wales, at a year old, wore a round cap of purple velvet with a broad band of gold and was wrapped in a robe of the Stewart tartan. On his third birthday the Prince of Wales appeared at Windsor dressed in Highland costume for the benefit of Lord Glenlyon.[7] On his father's birthday in 1847 he appeared in a kilt to recite, rather indistinctly, a few lines from the *Lord of the Isles*.[8] At Balmoral, from 1848, the boys wore Highland dress in and out of doors.[9] These outfits were economically handed down the family. The one worn by the Prince of Wales in December 1849 was later used by Prince Alfred, Princess Helena and Princess Louise. The Highland dress worn by the Princes set a fashion that was to be immensely popular for little boys during the next three decades, while plaid dresses of wool, silk or poplin became all the rage for small girls. In the same way, the appearance of the Prince of Wales wearing a sailor suit at Osborne in 1846 began a fashion that has continued to this day.

Koberwein's portrait of the children of the Crown Princess, painted in November 1865, shows the elder Prussian Princes in full Highland

X *Old Balmoral Castle, the Queen and Prince's Sitting-room* by James Giles

Watercolour with bodycolour, signed and dated 1855, 30·2 × 45 cm, RL 19470

'The drawing-room has much comfort, but no splendour. The walls are covered with light-coloured chintz, with furniture and hangings to match' (*Illustrated London News*, 16 September 1848). Almost all this furniture was acquired with the house in 1848.

XI *New Balmoral Castle, the Drawing-room* by James Roberts

Watercolour, signed and dated September 1857, 26 × 38·3 cm, RL 19477

Lady Augusta Bruce saw the castle as the Queen and Prince were about to arrive for their first stay in the new apartments. Almost everything was complete: 'the carpets are Royal Stuart Tartan and green Hunting Stuart, the curtains, the former lined with red, the same dress Stuart and a few chintz with a thistle pattern, the chairs and sofas in the drawing room are 'dress Stuart' poplin. All highly characteristic and appropriate, but not all equally *flatteux* to the eye'.

X

XI

XII *The Gillies' Ball* by Egron Lundgren

Watercolour and bodycolour, 30·7 × 43 cm, RL 19531

A scene at the second of the annual gillies' balls ('very merry, gay and pretty'), held on 19 September 1859. The Queen said that the sword dance was 'danced really beautifully, by little Ld Mc Duff'.

XIII *Albert Edward, Prince of Wales, and Prince Alfred* by Sir William Ross

Watercolour, signed and dated 1847, 25·8 × 21·1 cm, RL 13818

The Queen watched Ross painting the boys in November 1847. The elder one wears Royal Stewart and the younger Dress Stewart tartan.

dress, almost certainly a present from their grandmother.[10] In 1867, on his third birthday, the Queen sent Prince Albert Victor, the Prince of Wales's eldest son, his first kilt. She explained that 'his petticoats must be taken off underneath, but he [had] better have additional warm drawers underneath whenever he wears it, to keep him from catching cold. That's as you children used to wear it'.[11] As late as October 1898, as a great-grandmother, she described in her Journal how 'dear little David appeared for the first time in a kilt I gave him, of which he is very proud, & in which he looked charming'.[12]

53   *Princess Victoria, later Queen* by Paul Fischer

Watercolour heightened with white, signed and dated 1819, 27 × 22.5 cm, RL 14186

Described at this age by her father, the Duke of Kent, as 'rather a pocket Hercules than a pocket Venus', the little Princess was painted at Kensington Palace in the dress that she wore to celebrate the Duke's birthday on 2 November 1819.

54   *Prince Adolphus of Mecklenburg-Strelitz* by Sir William Ross

Watercolour, signed and dated 1853, 27·2 × 19·7 cm, RL 13836

When the little Prince visited London with his parents in the early summer of 1853, the Queen gave him two Highland outfits from John and James Meyer of London and Edinburgh, for which she paid £40.4s. He played with the royal children and the Queen found him 'a dear Boy, good, amiable & merry'. She commissioned this watercolour of him wearing the smartest of his new outfits.

With this enthusiasm for Highland dress, it is no surprise that the Queen was fascinated when she saw it worn in Scotland on her first visit. She noted in her Journal that Lord Breadalbane's men wore Campbell tartan; the Marquis had, in fact, given orders that several hundreds of his men should wear Highland dress and *The Times* commented that the result would be 'novel and picturesque'. Despite the cartoon *Just Kilted* in *Punch* in 1844 (52),[13] Prince Albert does not seem to have worn Highland dress himself before September 1847 when, at Ardverikie, he 'put on a Royal Stuart kilt with a dark green doublet & plaid, pouch & dirk & his Garter over his stocking, looking so handsome, as my dear Treasure ever does'.[14] In the following year at Balmoral, the Queen noted that the Prince was late for dinner owing to his 'struggles to dress in his kilt'.[15] She herself frequently wore satin dresses of Hunting Stewart and plaid shawls or scarves of Royal or Dress Stewart tartan, as did her Ladies in Waiting.[16]

55 *Highlanders on a Hillside* by William Wyld

Watercolour over ink, signed, 19 × 25 cm

A sketch in the Prince of Wales's scrapbook, presumably given to him by Wyld in 1852. It shows Highlanders wearing different tartans and hardly looking as well turned out as the Queen would have liked.

The Queen was delighted that Lord Abercorn wore his kilt when he greeted her at Laggan in 1847. She was full of admiration for the splendid Highland dress of the time of George II that Cluny Macpherson wore on Prince Albert's birthday. Lady Canning, on the other hand, was not impressed by a great gathering of Cameron clansmen, who appeared in force, wearing plaids of different designs, when the Queen arrived at Fort William. She was staying at Achnacarry with Cameron of Lochiel and agreed with *The Times* that the clan did not look smart: 'unless a chief dresses his clan in Tartan at his own expense they must make a ragged appearance – & we know of one kilt only going from here & that was a drunken carpenter who begged for the table cover (a Locheil Plaid) off the drawing room table to put on his shoulders & in it he went'.[17] Many were as enthusiastic as the Queen about wearing Highland dress. In 1857 Lord Clarendon wrote of his dread of being made to wear a kilt on a visit to Blair Castle, which he believed was now required of all visitors.[18]

When she attended a service at Crathie Church on her first visit to Balmoral, the Queen thought it a great pity that the villagers were not wearing the kilt. The *Illustrated London News* reported that the Queen had made Stewart tartan the 'holiday uniform of the Highlanders in her service at Balmoral; their ordinary one being, in accordance with her wishes, a dress of the Border tartan, commonly called Shepherd Tartan'.[19] It became traditional that her retainers should be given annually, as part of their wages, a suit of clothes of Balmoral tweed. A furious memorandum came from the Queen, in 1870, when she found that some of her keepers had been wearing knickerbockers. She thought it not at all becoming and gave an order that keepers and gillies should all wear kilts. Only when they were sick or out deer-stalking were they given a special dispensation to put on trousers; otherwise they were to wear the Balmoral kilt and tweed jacket with the Balmoral bonnet, which, she reiterated, had always been the uniform of her retainers.[20]

The Balmoral tartan seems to have been designed by the Queen and Prince about 1850. The Queen painted Annie Macdonald, the jäger's daughter, wearing a plaid of the pattern over her head as a shawl in 1852. The following year the gillies and Princes in Haag's watercolours wear it (colour plates XIV, XVI-XVII on pp89, 107-108). The rugs on the tables in several interior views by James Giles and James Roberts are of the same design (48 and colour plate X on p71). The Princes and the keeper's sons wear it in two watercolours by Kenneth MacLeay (89, 90). The pattern was based on the sett of the Royal Stewart, but with the red ground changed to grey. The various twists and plies of black and white are said to be in imitation of the marled rocks of Deeside.[21] The tartan was always woven in two weights and qualities, one for the royal family and the other for the Queen's retainers. There have been slight variations in the pattern over the years.

56 *Queen Victoria at her Spinning-wheel* by Sir Joseph Edgar Boehm

Pencil, signed and dated 1869, 22·4 × 16·8 cm, with curved top, RL 14207

Drawn in January 1869 at Osborne, where Boehm was making a statuette of the Queen, sitting at her spinning-wheel with a favourite dog beside her. She found the young Hungarian sculptor a 'gentleman-like, clever, excessively modest, quiet person'. He had a series of sittings in January and February. Sir Henry Ponsonby thought the portrait good: 'He has made her like, without too jowly a look'. Since at least 1865 the Queen had enjoyed working at her spinning-wheel, eager to practise a Highland craft.

In September 1850, the Queen drove across the Dee and stopped at a small cottage belonging to a weaver named Anderson, who wove tartan plaids single-handed. She saw him working away industriously at his loom, on 'a pretty pattern, which he said was "for men's trousers"'. The cottage was full of wools of different colours ready to be woven and she ordered a scarf from the old man, who was only too pleased to explain his craft to her.[22] Two years later, Dr Robertson, the factor at Balmoral, was arranging to employ old women on the estate to spin woollen yarn at the Queen's behest; they were paid English wages for their labour. The yarn was to be made into cloth, from which warm clothing could be manufactured to give to the poor. Tartan was also being woven locally and dispatched to Windsor. Dr Robertson was delighted to arrange for as much shepherd plaid to be woven as necessary – 'It will be quite a God send to the poor ladies to keep them employed'. In 1855 508 yards and in 1862 535 yards of 'home manufactured shepherd tartan', were sent to Windsor, to be made into uniforms for the children of the keepers and labourers in Windsor Great Park, who attended a school at Cumberland Lodge. The project was short-lived, but useful while it lasted. By 1864 most of the old women who had spun the wool were dead and the weaver was said to be 'getting dottled' and unable to do his work properly.[23]

On her first visit to Balmoral the Queen was pleased to hear from one of her gillies that they all spoke Gaelic among themselves. 'I like talking to the people here, they are so simple & straightforward, & I like their curious Highland English'.[24] Full of good intentions, the Queen arranged that lessons in Gaelic should be made available for the estate workers. During the first winter of 1851, 110 would-be scholars enrolled their names; by the end of the winter, twenty or thirty were still attending. The lending library, set up in the Servants' Hall at Balmoral in 1859, was stocked with learned and worthy books selected by the royal landlords and flourished, especially in the early days. Over 200 came to the opening, many wading up to seven miles through snow to be present. The Queen was eager to help the needy on the estate; fuel, venison and oatmeal, as well as money, were given where necessary. Shoes were provided for a family of six children under ten years old, to enable them to walk to school. Later the Queen was to give educational bursaries for children of retainers and tenants from the proceeds of the sale of her *Leaves*.[25]

The prosperity at Balmoral was in marked contrast to the impoverishment of many of the old estates, where the Scottish laws of entail prohibited owners from selling any part of their lands to pay off encumbrances; as Charles Kingsley wrote, Balmoral and Birkhall were 'a little oasis in the wilderness'.[26] Many, like Lord Cockburn, realised that improvements could and would only be made when 'English purses' and the 'Southern supplanters of our banished, beggarly, but proud lairds' took over the running of many of the estates. At Balmoral there was inevitably a marked improvement in the standard of living for those working on the estate. Not only were the Queen and Prince consciously concerned for their welfare, but the influx of visitors on royal visits meant further employment.

The Queen attended Highland Games for the first time on Prince Albert's birthday, 26 August 1847, while she was staying at Ardverikie. The reporter of the *Illustrated London News* described the spectators as consisting mainly of 'peasantry': 'a good sprinkling clad in kilt and plaid, mostly all wearing some piece of tartan apparel – or badge

57 *The Sword Bearer to Sir Charles Forbes* by Carl Haag

Watercolour, dated September 1853, 50·4 × 35·2 cm, with curved top, RL 20746

Haag admired this picturesque figure, carrying his huge two-handed sword, in the procession at the Braemar Gathering. The artist was invited to the camp at Corrie Mulzie on the following day and sketched the henchman, giving him a much more romantic and less bedraggled appearance than that revealed by a contemporary photograph. Braemar Castle is seen in the background.

in the way of bonnet or heather – of the mountains.'[27] The Queen was interested in the contests; putting the stone, throwing the hammer, tossing the caber and running races. She admired the immense strength of the competitors. At Osborne the following summer, Eleanor Stanley, who was in Waiting, came upon Macdonald 'showing some Southrons how to throw the cabard, that is a tree, as we saw them try to do at Inverness; and I must say he himself did it very well.

58 *The Royal Family at the Braemar Gathering* by Carl Haag

Pencil and sepia wash, 12·7 × 17·7 cm, RL 21318 f4

Sir Charles Forbes greeting the Queen, Prince Albert and their children at the Gathering on 15 September 1853.

I daresay there will be some sports of the kind today'.[28] In the south there was an increasing interest in the Games, as in all things relating to Scotland. In June 1849 Queen Victoria attended a 'National Fête' in the park of Holland House, Kensington, organised by the Scottish Society to raise money for hospitals and schools in Scotland. It was the first time that such a fête had been held in England, and for a charitable cause. Many Highlanders, including those who had won prizes at Ardverikie, came south for the occasion.

At Balmoral in 1848, the Queen had attended the Braemar Gathering at Invercauld. 'All the country round meets for games & feats of strength & we are to see a great shew of kilts', wrote Lady Canning. The Braemar Highland Society, which organised the games, also encouraged the use of the Gaelic language and the wearing of Highland dress. It had developed from the Braemar Wrights Friendly Society, which was set up early in the century to assist the impoverished members of the community. Braemar, for hundreds of years a focal point for communications in the area, was a natural centre for the Gatherings. Traditionally, the first games were said to have been organised there in the eleventh century by Malcolm Canmore, the Scottish king whose statue was later to stand in the entrance hall at Balmoral.

When Carl Haag was at Balmoral in 1853, he was provided with a pony to ride to Braemar Castle and join the royal family at the Gathering. He made a number of pencil and sepia-wash sketches, while watching the games, reels and sword dances (57, 58). In the royal enclosure he was introduced to Landseer and the Aberdeen painter John Phillip. Six

years later, the Swedish artist Egron Lundgren was invited to spend about three weeks at Balmoral. A number of his sketches found a place in the Queen's Souvenir Albums and preparatory studies are in the Nationalmuseum, Stockholm. He drew the showing of stags, some landscapes and the gillies' ball, but his most important sketches illustrate the Highland fête on 22 September 1859 (59, 61-62).

In the previous week at Aberdeen the Prince Consort had given his inaugural address as President of the British Association for the Promotion of Science, attended by 2,500 members. It was arranged that some of them should come to Balmoral for the Braemar Gathering, which on this occasion was to be held at the castle. Three or four 'weighty omnibuses', each bearing forty 'philosophers and savants', drove over and the visitors were given a stand-up luncheon in the new ballroom. The Queen was relieved to find that those professors who were invited to stay the night after the fête were 'very amiable & unostentatious, in spite of their learning'. She described the Gathering: 'It was a beautiful sight in spite of the frequent slight showers which at first tormented us, and the very high, cold wind. There were gleams of sunshine, which, with the Highlanders in their brilliant and picturesque dresses, the wild notes of the pipes, the band, and the beautiful back-

59 *Members of the British Association Watching Highland Dancing* by Egron Lundgren

Watercolour over sepia ink, 17·5 × 30 cm, RL 19485

60 *Egron Lundgren* from the *Illustrated London News*.

ground of mountains, rendered the scene striking in the extreme'.[29] Lundgren was at hand to sketch the events and draw the competitors, whose appearance contrasted strangely with the learned spectators wearing top hats and carrying furled umbrellas.

The Queen continued to support the Braemar Highland Society with subscriptions and attendance at the Gatherings, although as the years go by one can detect a note of boredom in her Journal: 'Went off well, but, as usual, it was a very slow affair', or 'The Games & everything were just as usual, – always rather hanging fire'.[30] In 1874, however, when she heard that neither Colonel Farquharson, Lord Fife nor Lord Macduff intended to be present at the Games at Old Mar, she was furious: 'What is National is so valuable in these days of levelling, and of absence of all that is exclusively National in spirit or romantic or poetic – especially when the love of low sports – like Pigeon shooting, & of gambling &

61 *The Race* by Egron Lundgren

Watercolour heightened with white, 24·3 × 20·7 cm, RL 19488

The Queen described the race as 'a pretty wild sight, but the men looked very cold with their bare legs & nothing on but their shirts & kilts. They ran beautifully & when they came to receive the prize from me had their plaids wrapped round them'.

62   *Tossing the Caber* by Egron Lundgren
Watercolour, 24·3 × 20·7 cm, RL 19489

racing & new foolish & even cruel ones like Polo &c are on the increase
– that everything ought to be done to keep it up'. After this outburst,
Colonel Farquharson and Lord Macduff agreed to attend. The old
keeper John Grant is reported to have told Colonel Farquharson in plain
language that it was a shame for him to have let the Games decay, but
the Colonel had to bear much of the expense of the Gatherings and
found that other support was forthcoming only when a member of the
royal family was to be present.[31]

With the Queen's patronage and local patriotism, the Games continued. In 1887 the Braemar Gathering was held at Balmoral in honour
of the Jubilee and between three and four thousand people attended. It
was again held there in 1890, when the Queen's support gave it national
importance and special trains had to be run to carry the large crowds
from Aberdeen to Deeside.[32]

Chapter Five

'This Dear Paradise': Balmoral, 1853-60

On 8 September 1853 the Queen wrote to her half-brother, Charles, Prince of Leiningen, 'Your young protégé C.Haag is here – & going to begin today but imagine his losing <u>All</u> his things & <u>all</u> his Materials on the rail road!'[1] This is the first intimation of the arrival at Balmoral of the artist who was to paint for the Queen the pictures that best illustrate her Scottish holidays. The Queen's interest in the progress of Carl Haag's work emerges from the pages of her Journal, while the artist gives a unique record of working for the royal couple in his own diaries.[2]

Early in October 1852 Haag had been on a painting excursion to the Inner Riss Valley in the Tyrol. He had heard that the Prince of Leiningen owned a shooting-lodge close by the inn where he was staying, but thought little of it until he chanced to meet the Prince, riding home from a hunting expedition. On discovering that Haag was an artist, Prince Charles invited him to sketch the stag he had just shot. Haag followed the hunters and began his drawing, watched by the Prince, who urged him to finish the sketch before the sun moved round and then invited him to lunch. Haag apologised for his informal costume, but the Prince reassured him that at his shooting-lodge it was only the servants who wore white tie and tails. After enjoying an al-fresco meal together, the Prince examined Haag's sketches. The artist explained that he was planning to spend the winter in Rome and to return to London in the spring to exhibit his pictures. The Prince urged him to show his work to the Queen, as she particularly admired anything from the Tyrol. On discovering that his host was the Queen's half-brother, Haag at once suggested painting a picture of him for her.

As the Duke and Duchess of Saxe-Coburg-Gotha, Prince Albert's brother and sister-in-law, were to join Prince Charles at the shooting-lodge in a few days time, it was decided that Haag should paint the Prince and the Duke together, as his introduction to the English court (64). Although he worked hard during their visit, Haag failed to complete the painting before his sitters left. They took the watercolour with them and it was arranged that Haag should put the finishing touches to it in London the following spring.

After a busy winter working in Rome, Haag travelled to England with a portfolio of studies and eight pictures for exhibition. He reached London on 26 March 1853, uncertain how to gain an audience with the Queen. He chanced to meet Dominic Colnaghi, the art dealer, from whom he learned that Miss Skerrett had been trying to trace his whereabouts. Haag wrote at once to Dr Becker, the Prince's Librarian,

64 *Charles Emich, Prince of Leiningen, with Ernest II, Duke of Saxe-Coburg-Gotha* by Carl Haag

Watercolour with bodycolour and scraping out, signed and dated 1852, 76·2 × 101 cm, RL 17108

Haag painted both sitters and the huntsmen from life, and he was taken to a special site to draw the mountain background. When the Prince of Leiningen died in 1856, his mother, the Duchess of Kent, wanted a copy made from the head in this portrait, considering it the best existing likeness of him.

as a result of which he was summoned to the Palace and presented to Prince Albert. He was told that his painting of the two Princes in the Tyrol had been given to Queen Victoria for Christmas by the sitters. Haag could now retouch the picture and arrange to exhibit it at the Society of Painters in Watercolour. Queen Victoria was unable to receive Carl Haag as she was awaiting the birth of her eighth child, Prince Leopold, but she asked to see some of his studies and, from among the twenty-one that he sent, she copied several in watercolour.

When Haag received an invitation to accompany the royal party to Balmoral in the autumn, he could scarcely believe his luck. At the same time, he was elected a full member of the Society of Painters in Watercolour. He also had a friendly letter from the Prince of Leiningen, inviting him back to the Tyrol, and when the Duke and Duchess of Saxe-Coburg-Gotha visited London, Haag took them round the Water-colour Exhibition. They went with him to his house, where the Duke conferred upon him the honour of Court Painter and asked him to visit them in Coburg. This flood of good fortune caused Haag's friends to tease him; only he, they said, could obtain an introduction at court by going to an almost totally inaccessible valley in the Tyrol and, on his return to England, find himself sought out by the Queen's art publishers with an offer of further preferment.

At Balmoral Haag began work on 8 September, in the Iron Ballroom. At first he had to use some of the Queen's own painting materials, until his own, which he had lost on the railway journey north, were traced and returned to him. The Iron Ballroom was arranged as a studio (63), but it was not designed to be heated or to have artificial light. On a hot day the sun on the metal roof made it unbearable and by late September it had become so cold that Haag was allowed the use of a room in a nearby cottage when he needed a fire.

At his first interview with the Queen, Haag was left in no doubt that he was expected to work hard and fast, which he was only too anxious to do; he was convinced that royal favour and patronage would make his fortune. His first job was to illustrate a salmon-spearing, or leistering, which took place on the River Dee the day after his arrival (65 and colour plate XIV on p89). After a wet start to the day, the weather cleared and Haag set off to the river to see the sport. He found that the Queen, the Princesses and ladies of the court had already arrived on the opposite bank. As soon as she saw Haag the Queen sent John Macdonald to carry the artist across to their side. When he gained the bank, the painter had at once to show his sketches to the Queen, who suggested other places from which he should draw.

Meanwhile the beaters waded in the river with fishing nets wound round poles, disturbing the water and urging the salmon to swim upstream. About a mile further up the river more beaters, armed with poles, were banging on the rocks so that the frightened fish would turn back towards the nets which barred their escape. As they swam back,

Prince Albert, his two eldest sons and some of the gentlemen attempted to spear the salmon from the rocks, armed with iron tridents or leisters with barbed prongs; the Prince succeeded in spearing three. Haag sketched all morning. When the leistering was over, he went back to work in the Iron Ballroom. He had hoped to persuade some of the beaters to pose for him in the afternoon, but they had eaten and drunk far too much after their exertions and were in no fit state to sit to him that day. He had to wait four days before he could draw his models.

On the eve of the royal departure, Haag was struggling to paint in the Iron Ballroom among half-packed trunks and chests, when the Queen came to ask him to paint a 'secret picture' of the leistering as a birthday present for Prince Albert. It was to show John Macdonald in the water with the Prince of Wales and Prince Alfred. Haag was so delighted with the idea that he 'jumped for joy' after the Queen had left. He went off at once to the billiard-room to make studies of the Princes. Prince Albert came in to watch him at work and assured him

65   *Salmon Spearing in the River Dee* by Carl Haag

Watercolour and scraping out, 27·2 × 39·2 cm, RL 20762

A study for the background of colour plate XIV on p89.

66 *Lizzie Stewart and Mary Symons* by
Carl Haag

Watercolour with bodycolour and
scraping out, dated October 1853,
50·5 × 35 cm, with curved top, RL 20747

One of Haag's first commissions from the
Queen on his arrival at Balmoral was to
draw the small daughters of her forester
and the village shopkeeper, whom she
had herself drawn three years previously.
Haag worked all day, from nine o'clock in
the morning until evening to finish the
portraits.

67 *Lizzie Stewart and Mary Symons* by
Queen Victoria (detail)

Watercolour, signed and dated 1850,
20·6 × 27·5 cm, RL K 27 f75

that his new paintings would greatly enhance his reputation, especially if they were later engraved.

Throughout the previous month Prince Albert had been full of suggestions and instructions for the layout of Haag's first big commission, a picture to be called *Evening at Balmoral* or *Showing the Stags by Torchlight* (4, 69, 71, 79 and colour plates XV, XVI on pp90, 107). On 10 September Haag received orders to draw a ten-point stag, shot the previous day by Prince Albert. He sat in the wet grass working on his study for four hours, until he was benighted. The Prince, meanwhile, was out on another expedition and shots could be heard in the distance. At nine o'clock Haag was summoned to the castle and, after they had dined, the royal party emerged from the main entrance to see the stags that had been killed displayed by torchlight. The Queen was wearing a black cloak and a splendid tiara; the ladies were tightly wrapped in shawls and Prince Albert wore Highland dress. It was just such a 'showing' as had excited the Queen at Taymouth and Blair Castle, which she had described to Haag as a splendid subject for a painting on their first meeting. When the scene was re-enacted two evenings later, Colonel Gordon, the Prince's Equerry, helped Haag to arrange the stags and torch-bearers so that he could begin to lay out his composition.

A few days later Haag began a drawing of the entrance front of the castle for the background to his picture (colour plate XV on p90). Although it was only to appear in darkness, Haag made a fully coloured study of the house. There were constant interruptions while he worked. The Queen came to discuss the difference between the Tyrolese Alps and the Highland mountains, the royal children to watch him at work and to talk to him. The Princess Royal was to write to Prince Charles that Haag 'seems a very clever artist' and had made 'some extremely pretty drawings'.[3] Haag admired her clear mind and quick understanding. Finally it began to rain and Haag had to seek refuge in the Iron Ballroom. The next day he tried to complete his watercolour of the outside of the house, but the wind was too strong and he could not work. On returning to the Ballroom, he found that the royal children, their tutor and the Ladies in Waiting were all being taught to dance reels. The following day, with an improvement in the weather, Haag again began to paint out of doors, but the Queen arrived with copies that she had been making from his studies, which she wished to discuss with him. The next morning, work was again impossible because Dr Becker planned to take photographs to help Haag with the picture. Groups of royal sitters were arranged by the front door. Unfortunately, only two of Dr Becker's calotypes were successful.

On 26 September, two weeks after he had begun working on the design, the Queen and Prince called Haag to the conservatory (70) to examine his sketches and discuss his composition. With their approval secured, he spent the afternoon laying out a full-scale cartoon. When

Opposite
XIV   *Salmon Leistering in the River Dee: the Prince of Wales and Prince Alfred, Guided by John Macdonald, Returning from the Salmon Spearing* by Carl Haag

Watercolour and scraping out, signed and dated 1854, 50·4 × 35·5 cm, with curved top, RL 22057

Haag's full-scale cartoon for this picture, in pencil with some watercolour, is also in the Royal Collection.

68   *Carl Haag*

A calotype taken by Dr Becker in October 1853. The artist is holding a photograph of the recently completed portrait of Prince Arthur by Winterhalter.

XIV

XV   *Old Balmoral Castle, the South Front*
by Carl Haag

Watercolour, 35 × 50·4 cm, RL 20769

A study for *Evening at Balmoral* and one of
the best surviving records of the
appearance of the old castle, soon to be
destroyed. Originally all thirty-four of
Haag's studies for *Morning* and *Evening at
Balmoral* were mounted together in an
album entitled *Original Studies from
Nature in the Highlands, 1853.* Ten days
after the death of the Prince Consort, the
Queen sent for this book from the library
at Windsor Castle, perhaps so that she
could dwell on the past.

69 A study for *Evening at Balmoral* by Carl Haag

Pencil, 12·7 × 17·7 cm, RL 21318 f32v

An early stage in the evolution of the composition, for which several studies exist.

the Prince returned from a successful day's shooting, he was full of praise. The dead stags were again shown by torchlight and the next day one was brought into the Iron Ballroom for Haag to paint. The royal family kept looking in to watch his progress, but they found the smell of the disembowelled animal almost unbearable. Haag, who had never painted animals before, was proud of his efforts, but admitted to the Prince that he would never be a Landseer. He worked all day, despite the smell, and in the afternoon the Queen joined him to sketch the stag herself. Haag was much impressed by her speed and accuracy and found her kind and friendly. The Queen's drawings, with Dr Becker's photographs of the stags' heads, were put into special 'Stag Books', in which the Prince's trophies were recorded.[4]

Everything was done to help Haag with his work. When he wished to go sketching, a pony with a servant was ordered to carry his equipment. Dr Becker had orders to photograph anything Haag wished (72, 74); he encouraged the artist by assuring him he was a great success

with the whole court and that none of his predecessors had been so well received. Haag was delighted and broke into such an ecstatic dance that he sprained his leg. His work was not completed without incident: when Colonel Gordon was sitting for his portrait, the rain came through the roof and onto the artist's paper; another time, his stool broke and he landed, much shaken, on the floor, to the amusement of the Queen when she heard the story at dinner.

The subject of Carl Haag's other large watercolour, *Morning in the Highlands* or the *Ascent of Lochnagar*, was planned after an expedition up that mountain (1, 73, 75-76 and colour plate XVII on p108). Lochnagar, nearly 4,000 feet high, lay on the Balmoral estate to the south of the castle. The Queen called it 'the jewel of all the mountains here'[5] and it presented a challenge every year for a good day's excursion. The theme had been in the Queen's mind as a subject for a picture since her expedition up Glen Tilt in 1844. She was anxious that Haag should 'see all' and on 17 September, before he was out of bed, he received orders from the castle to be at the Falls of the Garbh Allt by ten o'clock.

70 *Old Balmoral Castle, the Conservatory* by William Wyld

Watercolour, signed and dated 1852, 22·9 × 33·5 cm, RL 19481

The position of the conservatory, with its curved exterior wall can be seen in plate 38 and colour plate XV on p90.

71 *George, 4th Earl of Aberdeen* by Carl Haag

Pencil with watercolour, 35 × 25 cm, RL 17165

A study for *Evening at Balmoral*, in which the Prime Minister appears behind Prince Albert. In fact Lord Aberdeen did not go to Balmoral during the visit of 1853, so the study was presumably made in London. The Queen must have been particularly anxious that he should appear in the picture because of his associations with the castle. On his death, she wrote that he was 'one of the few remaining experienced & truly loyal public men, who would never tolerate any dishonourable proceedings, straight-forward, highminded, the kindest of friends, so wise in his opinions' (Journal, 14 December 1860).

A tweed suit, which Haag had been told to have made on his arrival at Balmoral the previous week, had not yet been delivered so he set off in his dark suit. When he joined the royal party the Queen was amused by his appearance, but the Prince was horrified and at once lent Haag a grey plaid of his own to wear.

The expedition moved off in almost the order that Haag was later to show in his painting. He himself rode behind the royal party on a black horse. After him came the servants, gillies and a pony laden with

A calotype taken by Dr Becker on
3 October 1853 for Haag's use.

73 *Prince Albert's Pony, Held by a Gillie*
by Carl Haag

Watercolour and scraping out, signed and
dated 1853, 25 × 35 cm, RL 20764

A study for *Morning in the Highlands*, of
the pony ridden by the Prince up the steep
mountain track. It shows how Haag used
photographs and careful preliminary
watercolour studies before embarking on
his final picture.

provisions. Haag was particularly pleased by the sight of the procession
winding up the hillside and was eager to paint such a scene. This
delighted the Prince who said it was the Queen's dearest wish that he
should do so. As they climbed higher and higher, Prince Albert made
suggestions for the composition. Finally they all reached the top of the

74   *Carl Haag with the Prince's Dogs*

A calotype taken by Dr Becker on
3 October 1853. The artist wears the
new grey tweed suit specially made for
him at Balmoral.

75   *Albert Edward, Prince of Wales* by
Carl Haag

Pencil, 25·3 × 17·7 cm, with curved
corners, RL 17039

A study for *Morning in the Highlands* .

mountain and, while lunching on the summit, were much impressed
by the wonderful views to be seen in all directions, as the cold mist
drifted away (97). They returned home by a different route, the Queen
descending the first 900 feet on foot down a steep, rough, dry walk.

The Prince set off stalking deer and he invited Haag to follow him.
The artist watched while the Prince's hounds attacked a stag on a steep
hillside; then, as it fell into a stream, the hounds were called off so
that the Prince could dispatch it and Haag helped him to pull out the
carcass by the antlers. Riding home together, Prince Albert talked to
Haag with knowledge and sympathy of the arts and of artists, until
they parted at the riverbank.

During the days that followed, Haag fixed up a large sheet of paper
for the new project and had much discussion about the composition
with Prince Albert, who drew out his idea for the design with a stick
in some sand. Haag was depressed because he felt he had achieved so
little during his visit, but the Prince consoled him by saying that it was
impossible to do two things at once and that Haag had been so busy
absorbing all he was seeing on this, his first visit to Scotland, that he
could not 'give out' at the same time; he would produce excellent
things when he had assimilated all the new impressions. Haag was
greatly encouraged and went up to the castle the next morning with
renewed enthusiasm, only to find that the Prince had gone out stalking
and the Queen for a drive; there was no one available to sit for him,
accompany him on a sketching expedition or carry his materials. He

76 *Jamie Gow with the Provision Pony, Jock Wemyss* by Carl Haag

Watercolour and scraping out, 35 × 50 cm, RL 20752

A study for *Morning in the Highlands*. Carl Haag chose Jamie Gow, 'a little fellow like Sancho Panza', with cheeks that glowed like ripe apples, to act as his model for the man leading the provision pony up Lochnagar. Gow worked on the estate and, with difficulty owing to his small stature, rang the bells and dug the graves in Crathie churchyard. He was greatly excited at the prospect of achieving immortality in a painting to be hung in a royal palace. John Grant, who seldom smiled, shook with laughter at the idea of Gow having a prominent place in the picture. Sadly for Gow, another gillie replaced him in the final painting.

returned sadly to the Iron Ballroom to continue work, again to be distracted, as so often, by the children's Scottish reels.

Prince Albert wanted Haag to complete the *Morning in the Highlands* as a Christmas present for the Queen, so the artist decided not to visit Italy or return to the Riss Valley. His decision delighted the Queen. Her activities at Balmoral would now be really effectively depicted by this 'most good natured, good humoured clever & agreeable little man'.[6]

Each year, at the end of the Scottish holiday, the thought of her return to the south plunged the Queen in gloom. Writing on her return to Windsor to Feodora, Princess of Hohenlohe-Langenburg, she explained: 'I pine for my dear Highlands wh: I get more attached to every year. The life here is so different; it is so formal to what it is there!', and she quoted Byron's early poem:

'England! thy beauties are tame & domestic
To one who has roved o'er the Mountains afar;
Oh for the Crags that are wild & majestic!
The steep frowning glories of dark Loch na Gar!'[7]

This passion for Balmoral did not go unnoticed by the Queen's subjects. Every action of the royal family was reported daily in the Court Circular. *The Daily News* carried an article contrasting 'the simple annals of the tranquil and rational life led by our beloved QUEEN at Balmoral' with 'the feverish and nightmare existence of continental sovereigns'. They considered her fortunate to be able to withdraw to the seclusion of Balmoral, where 'beauty smiles in the lap of terror', and to let the world pass by while she enjoyed the felicity of her private life.[8]

In fact, although the Queen seemed far removed from the problems of domestic politics and international crises, she kept abreast of the affairs of the nation. Her Journal in that autumn of 1853 is full of anxious comment about the looming conflict in the Crimea. 'One Crown alone', she would have read in *The Times*, 'sits securely upon its wearer's head...She is now reaping the reward of her Spotless life – of her anxiety for the public welfare – of her daily endeavour to identify her rule with the best interests of her people'.[9] When Turkey declared war on Russia, the Queen cut short her holiday in Scotland – 'duty of course goes before everything'[10] – and returned to London on 13 October.

Carl Haag, meanwhile, had no such worries. His two large projects were keeping him busy. He was up at five-thirty every morning and at work in the Iron Ballroom by eight o'clock. On the day of the gillies' ball, he found himself banished, while preparations were being made for the dance. He went out to draw a distant view of Lochnagar, but was so plagued by midges that he sent his servant back to the inn for some cigars. He smoked nine, although six weeks previously he claimed to have given up smoking.

When the Queen and Prince paid him a last visit, she urged the artist to be particularly careful of his paintings and to be sure not to mislay anything on his journey south. After the court had left, Haag stayed on for a further nine days to work, but the house seemed dead and the few remaining servants crept about quietly. Prince Albert had arranged for John Grant to supply Haag with all he needed. He was given the best horse in the stable and felt himself to be almost 'Master of Balmoral'. He made sketches of the ponies, the Prince's hounds, John Grant and the gillies. The House Steward in the castle, the Alsatian François d'Albertançon, wept on Haag's departure. He felt, he said, like an exile with no one left to talk to.

On his return to London, Carl Haag continued work on the pictures. *Morning in the Highlands* was completed and given to the Queen by the Prince for Christmas. Haag took *Evening at Balmoral* to Windsor Castle in November and to Buckingham Palace in April 1854, so that the Queen could sit for her portrait. She thought it a very beautiful picture and realised that Haag had worked hard. It was to be a present from the Queen to the Prince on his birthday in August, but both paintings were completed for exhibition at the Society of Painters in Watercolour in the spring of 1854. At the Royal Academy in May of that same year, Sir Edwin Landseer showed his large unfinished *Royal Sports on Hill and Loch*. The liveliness of his first oil sketch had evaporated. The figures were static and the likenesses embarrassingly bad; a sad contrast to Haag's competent, well-composed and highly finished watercolours.

Haag's efforts seem to have fulfilled the Queen's needs for a time. For the next five years, no artist was summoned to Balmoral during the royal residence. Colebrooke Stockdale was paid for two views in 1856, but did not stay at the castle (colour plate XVIII on p117). Carlo Bossoli seems to have been visiting Sir James Clark's son in October 1856, when the Queen and Prince 'looked over some charming sketches'.[11] It was perhaps on this occasion that they acquired one each (colour plate XIX on p117). The pattern of the royal holidays continued. The Princess Royal married in 1858 and the following year her mother wrote to her, saying that she was enjoying herself more than ever at Balmoral that autumn. She had been out for the day on seventeen occasions and up on the hills in all directions. She had overcome all her nervousness on the hill ponies, chiefly through the 'extreme attention, care & handiness of good, faithful J. Brown, – than whom I have no better or more intelligent Servant anywhere'.[12]

Lundgren was the artist in residence at Balmoral in the autumn of 1859 and the next year George Fripp was invited. The Queen and

77 View of New Balmoral Castle from across the Dee by George A. Fripp

Watercolour heightened with white, signed and dated 1860, 30·3 × 48·4 cm, RL 19638

The new castle complete with the grounds laid out by the Prince. His extensive afforestation of the estate meant that this clear view was soon to be obscured.

78 *Glen Derry* by George A. Fripp

Watercolour with scraping out, signed,
30·3 × 47·4 cm, RL 19637

The Queen made several visits to this wild
glen, commenting on the remains of a
splendid forest and riding up the rough
track towards Loch Etchachan, with Ben
Macdui visible on the left.

Prince Albert had bought watercolours by Fripp in the 1840s and a
large view of Kilchurn Castle in 1852.[13] Apparently without warning
he was summoned to Osborne on 23 July 1860 and received an invitation to go to Scotland the following week, with a commission to
make eight finished watercolours of the scenery around Balmoral. On
his return to London that evening, Fripp called on his friend Carl
Haag, who was delighted to hear the news. He knew that Fripp's wife
was expecting their ninth child and that the royal commission would
greatly ease his financial difficulties.

On 1 August Fripp set off for Balmoral. He stayed in a hostelry at
Inver, on Haag's recommendation, and later at Braemar. After the
royal party left in mid-September, Fripp stayed on for another fort-
night, hoping in vain for sufficiently fine weather to reach and paint
Loch Avon. For a week or more before he left, the higher mountains were covered with snow and the whole area was under snow by
10 October. He hoped to be invited back the following year, perhaps
earlier in the season. He felt that his pictures were as good as the cold

and uncertain weather had allowed. He had been given all facilities and a pony whenever he needed one; but the weather on Deeside that year, even in August, had been most unfavourable for sketching.[14]

On his return south, Fripp made the crucial mistake of carrying out his finished watercolours on a larger scale than the pattern given to him by the Queen (77, 78). While he was at Balmoral she had increased her order from eight to twelve paintings. In November he dispatched the completed pictures, mounted in a folio, and apologised for the increase in size, saying he thought they would lose much by being cut down. He explained that 'owing to the weakness and shortness of my sight (though I ever carried a small opera glass with me) I am not able to do justice to subjects requiring much careful drawing, and of great range...slight sketches appear to me insufficient in many cases to express the character of Scotch scenery'.[15] Fripp was paid £150 and Haag found him busy and happy, having heard that the watercolours had pleased the Queen. Fripp did not, as he had hoped, receive an invitation to return to Balmoral the following year.

Writing after the Prince's death about the watercolours in her Souvenir Albums, the Queen explained that the Prince 'was not satisfied if they were not really good (wh. sometimes disappointed me – as I – stupidly – & unworthily – was more easily satisfied with mediocrity').[16] The Prince had been 'much disappointed with Fripp's views in the Highlands taken last year'; and apart from a view of Penrhyn Castle, made on his way south from Balmoral, Fripp received no more commissions from the Queen. His only other work in the Royal Collection is an insignificant little watercolour given to the Queen at her Jubilee in 1887, with those by other members of the Royal Society of Painters in Watercolour.

Chapter Six

After the Death of the Prince

'He who was the <u>moving</u> power of <u>all</u>, He on whom I lent for 22 years – He <u>taken</u> – & I – who <u>am</u> fit for nothing <u>alone</u>, who constantly feel as if I ought not to be here – am <u>left</u> – half wild with grief!'[1] Queen Victoria's first visit to Balmoral, 'Here – <u>where all</u> was made for Him – where the life was <u>one</u> of activity',[2] after the shattering blow of her husband's death in December 1861 was a formidable test of her strength. It was raining on her arrival at the castle on 2 May 1862 and there was 'not a soul out – only Dr Robertson at the door and poor Grant in the hall! Oh! darling child', she wrote to the Crown Princess, 'the agonising sobs as I crawled up with Alice and Affie! The stag's heads – the rooms – blessed, darling Papa's room – then his coats – his caps – kilts – all, all convulsed my poor shattered frame!'[3] At his first interview with the Queen, Dr Robertson found her in the Prince's room, with several articles of dress and other things that had belonged to him.

The Queen forced herself to take an interest in the estate, to continue the work of her beloved husband. She gave orders that there was to be no shooting that year; the Prince's forest was to remain perfectly quiet. Two weeks after her arrival at Balmoral, Dr Robertson found the Queen able to speak of the late Prince without 'painful bursts of grief as formerly'.[4] Charles Dickens understood that 'in the Highlands the queen saw more of her beloved prince than elsewhere: walking with him, riding with him, reading with him, or sketching by his side continually',[5] so it was at Balmoral that his absence was felt perhaps more than anywhere else. The Queen was convinced at first that she could not, and would not, long outlive her husband: 'It cannot, I am sure it will <u>not last</u> & those blessed Arms will receive me very shortly, <u>never</u> <u>to part</u>'.[6] Little did she know that half her life was still before her.

Chapter heading:
79   *Head of Prince Albert* by Carl Haag

RL 21318 f27v

A study for *Evening at Balmoral*.

At first she could think only of setting up memorials to the Prince. At once she began to plan the Mausoleum at Frogmore and commissioned artists to paint copies of existing portraits or to colour photographs of the Prince. Theed worked both on a posthumous bust and, by February 1862, on a full-scale statue of the Prince in Highland dress for Balmoral (80). When the Queen went north in May, Edward Corbould, who had been colouring photographs of the Prince for her since February, went too (99). Her principal interest on her first visit was in an obelisk, which was to be erected to his memory by the people on the estate, but she also turned back to the painters whose work had given them so much pleasure during their happy days together in Scotland.

Both William Leitch and his son, Richard, had been at Balmoral in the autumn of 1861, teaching and painting for the Queen. When they were next summoned to Deeside in August 1862, the situation was very different. The elder Leitch described the atmosphere in a letter: 'The Queen is still the kind, good, and gracious lady that she always was, but I need hardly tell you that there is a change. Indeed the whole place is changed. Everything very quiet and still. How

80 *The Unveiling of the Statue of the Prince Consort at Balmoral on 15 October 1867* by George H. Thomas

Watercolour, 28·6 × 45 cm, RL 22061

A statue of the Prince by William Theed, criticised and corrected at each stage of its making by the Queen, had been set up at the foot of the staircase in the castle on 15 August 1862. George Thomas, who had worked extensively in the south for the Queen over the previous twelve years, was asked to attend and draw the ceremony at which this second colossal version in bronze was unveiled. It proved to be Thomas's last work for her, as he died the following year. On the right can be seen the new dairy, built after the Prince's death, and on the left the pyramid erected to his memory in 1862.

different from my first visit here — the joyous bustle in the morning when the Prince went out: the highland ponies and the dogs; the gillies and the pipers. Then the coming home — the Queen and her ladies going out to meet them, and the merry time afterwards; the torch-light sword-dancers on the green, and the servants' ball closing the day. Now all is gone with him who was the life and soul of it all'.[7]

In 1860 and 1861 the Queen and Prince had taken part in a series of excursions, which they called the 'Great Expeditions'. They travelled long distances, sometimes over two days, breaking the journeys by staying *incognito* at local inns. The Queen, who had been overwhelmed by the death of her mother in March 1861, found that the long expeditions in the open air helped her to recover her strength. By the end of that holiday she felt able to bear any fatigue. Now the Queen was anxious to capture for posterity some memories of those excursions. She wrote to Princess Alice on 28 August: 'You know that good old Mr. Leitch has been here for 3 weeks & both Lenchen & Louise colour charmingly. The younger Leitch has been to Blair to make Sketches of our dear dear Expeditions & is going to make all the remaining views wh. I can never photograph'.[8] In fact, George Washington Wilson had already been sent to make photographic views, but this did not completely satisfy the Queen. William Leitch was not physically fit to travel the distances required, so his son retraced the routes of the 'Great Expeditions' and painted a series of watercolours (81-84 and colour plate XXI on p119). They were used, not only to complete

81 *The Ramsay Arms, Fettercairn* by Richard P. Leitch

Watercolour, heightened with white, signed and dated 1863, 20·7 × 42·3 cm, RL 19657

On the night of 20 September 1861, on their second 'Great Expedition', the royal party travelled forty miles from Balmoral and slept at this inn. The identity of their guests was revealed to the landlord and his wife, but to 'no one else except the coachman, and they kept the secret admirably'. This secrecy added to the Queen's enjoyment, but unfortunately the beds at the inn were so hard that she slept badly.

82   *The Farm at Dalwhinnie* by Richard P.Leitch

Watercolour heightened with white, signed and dated 1862, 20·6 × 41 cm, RL 19656

83   *Crossing the Falls of the Poll Tarff* by Richard P.Leitch

Watercolour heightened with white, and scraping out, 28 × 45·4 cm, RL 19686

On the third 'Great Expedition', to Glen Feshie and Blair Castle, the royal party spent the night of 8 October 1861 at Dalwhinnie. The royal baggage is shown being unpacked. The visitors paid the penalty of travelling *incognito*: 'the worst was there was hardly anything to eat, only tea which I cannot take at night & 2 miserable starved Highland chickens. It certainly was not a nice, or very appetising supper', wrote the Queen, 'No pudding, and no fun'.

In Leitch's reconstruction of the royal party crossing the ford at the confluence of the rivers Tarff and Tilt, the falls are much less dramatic than in Carl Haag's record of the scene (colour plate XX on p118).

the Souvenir Albums, but also later as plates in her *Leaves from the Journal of Our Life in the Highlands.*

In 1863 William Leitch was once more at Balmoral and teaching for thirty days at four guineas a day. To his delight, the Queen began to paint again, which she had not done with him since the Prince's death. In a letter of 30 September, Leitch wrote of a drawing party held out of doors with Princess Alice: 'We got on very well, and the Queen was cheerful and enjoyed the work – chatting, and occasionally laughing at the little difficulties and drawbacks, and speaking also of auld lang syne in a very feeling manner, so that nearly two hours went by in a most interesting and delightful way imaginable'.[9] He described to his wife an expedition made a week later with 'her Majesty on a rough Highland pony with a Highlander to lead it; Lady Churchill walking alongside of the Queen; and Princess Louise also trudging along, and your husband walking alongside of the Princess. When we got to our place of work there was another picture – her Majesty sitting in the middle of a country road, with a great rough stone out of the river to put her paint box on; Lady Churchill holding an umbrella over the Queen's head, and I seated near her Majesty so that she could see what I was doing. The Princess Louise was on my right hand, sitting on a big stone, and working away at her drawing, and the Highlander – the Queen's personal attendant, John Brown – with the pony in the background. Several people that passed did, I assure you, stare at the group. The Queen evidently enjoyed it very much. There was lots of talking and laughing, and nearly two hours passed away very soon – the Queen remarking how quickly the time flew when she was drawing'.[10] The Queen's own impression of her visit to Balmoral that year is in marked contrast: 'Left without any one to cheer my loneliness here, when I am now so very peculiarly forlorn here',[11] she wrote to the Crown Princess. The season was 'dreadful' and 'All the interest for sport and expeditions gone, so that all about sport is kept from me, for I wince under it'.[12]

William Leitch was at Balmoral during the whole of the royal visit, available to give lessons whenever required or to accompany sketching parties, looking, as the Queen put it, 'wonderful & not at all happy on his pony'.[13] Most of the younger members of the royal family seem to have enjoyed lessons with him, but Prince Arthur, despite frequent wet days which kept him indoors, apparently availed himself of Leitch's presence on only one occasion. Leitch sent him drawings to copy and praised his beautiful straight lines, but at thirteen he seems to have felt that there were more amusing things to do at Balmoral than draw with his sisters.

Apparently neither of the Leitchs returned to Balmoral after 1863. The following year, William continued to teach the Queen and her children in the south, although he now had no other pupils. In 1864 he was granted an annuity by her. The last time he taught the Queen

was in April 1865. At the studio sale after his death in 1883, the Queen acquired many works by her 'kind old Drawing Master', examples of the sketches and unfinished studies that she so much admired. Some of these had been made during Leitch's last visits to Balmoral.[14]

In August 1862, while Richard Leitch was travelling about Scotland and drawing the places that the Queen had visited the previous autumn, the historian and essayist Arthur Helps was staying at the castle in his capacity as Clerk of the Privy Council. He was also discussing with the Queen an edition of the Prince's *Speeches and Addresses*, which he was editing for publication. During the visit, she allowed Helps to read part of her Journal and suggested that a selection of extracts, relating to the visits to Scotland between 1848 and 1861, might be privately printed for her family and chosen friends. The Queen found Helps sympathetic, 'a clever, kind good, warm hearted man'[15] and as his admiration for Prince Albert was 'unbounded', they proceeded together to annotate and edit parts of the Journal.

By December 1864, the Queen was finding it 'quite an interest'[16] to watch the progress of the book and by the following March she was very busy looking through the final set of proofs. By the end of May, she had nearly finished and the first edition of the *Leaves from the Journal of Our Life in the Highlands* was printed that year. There were just sixty-three copies. The Queen gave one to the Prince of Wales on

84   *Blair Castle with the Boat Carriage* by Richard P. Leitch

Watercolour heightened with white, signed and dated 1863, 20·7 × 42 cm, RL 19655

At Blair, the Queen drove in the Duke's carriage, 'a very peculiar one, viz., a boat – a mere boat (which is very light), put on four wheels, drawn by a pair of horses with a postilion'. A nostalgic drive up Glen Tilt followed, as far as Forest Lodge, where ponies awaited them for the ride to the ford of the Poll Tarff.

XVI *Evening at Balmoral* by Carl Haag

Watercolour, signed and dated 1854,
76·5 × 133·3 cm, with curved top,
RL 22033

Lord Aberdeen and Sir Charles Phipps
stand behind the Prince. The Duchess of
Kent and three Ladies in Waiting are
behind the Queen and the Prince of
Wales. On the right, Count Alexander
Mensdorff stands with Colonel Alexander
Gordon. When this picture was exhibited
in 1854, the critics were full of praise: the
Illustrated London News found the
execution of the details in both of Haag's
pictures 'admirable, and the colouring
clean and luminous'. *The Athenaeum*, a
journal often critical of Haag's work, said:
'Carl Haag has surpassed himself, if not
most of his predecessors, in his two
companion pictures'. It praised 'Prince
Albert whose attitude is noble and
manly'. The review then described the

three sources of light in the picture: first
from the windows illuminating the
gentlemen in the centre; second from the
bundle of burning pine-staves held by the
gillie John Brown, seen back-view, 'whose
strong glow of light struggles with the full
blue moonlight, whose pale shadows
contrast with those crimsoned by the
flame. A third light, that of the drawing-
room, blends with these two, while the
whole picture is bathed in a golden
universal tone, very beautiful, but we
think more resembling that of lamplight
than the lurid fitful catching spurts
produced by torches. For sin, however, in
so beautiful an aspect, we confess to have
some sympathy, and prefer an artistic
falsehood to a disgusting truth. The light
and shade is daring in the extreme,
statuesque and firm, and the drawing very
perfect. The whole picture has a regal air
about it, and is fit for any palace in
Christendom' (29 April 1854).

XVII *Morning in the Highlands* by Carl Haag

Watercolour, signed and dated 1853, 77 × 133·6 cm, with curved top, RL 22032

The royal party start out to ascend Lochnagar, the mountain in the distance. John Grant and a gillie head the procession, followed by Prince Albert. Princess Alice and Prince Alfred precede the Queen, while the Princess Royal and the Prince of Wales follow with the Hon. Mary Bulteel (who later married Colonel Henry Ponsonby). When this picture was shown at the Society of Painters in Watercolour during the spring of 1854, the reviewer in the *Illustrated London News* noted that 'considerable ability has been displayed in the arrangement of a rather difficult subject; not however, without betraying some symptoms of effort': a considerable understatement in view of Haag's only too-conscious efforts over the last months. The critic in *The Athenaeum* waxed lyrical over this picture, where all are seen 'struggling up round the crags of Byron's favourite mountain, down whose broad steeps the flowers of the heather are streaming like purple wine down the hills at the vintage...The richness of colour and its lucidity carry this painting into a region quite distinct from all the indefinite blurrings that were called water-colour drawings in the days of our fathers'.

24 September 1865, which she inscribed as 'This account of our happy life, now for ever past & of his happy Childhood'. There were a number of plates based on photographs, the Queen's engraved writing-paper headings and Richard Leitch's watercolours.[17] The Queen was immensely proud of 'my poor little Highland book – my only book',[18] and was overcome by the affectionate and loyal reception it received. Her children, although they dared not tell her so, deeply disapproved of this exposure of their private lives, even to their immediate circle, but the success of the project merely encouraged the Queen to further literary endeavour.

She wrote to the Crown Princess: 'It was so much liked, that I was begged & asked to allow it to be published – the good Dean of Windsor amongst other wise & kind people – saying it wld., from its simplicity & the kindly feelings expressed to those below us – do so much good. I therefore consented – cutting out some of the more familiar descriptions, & being subjected by Mr Helps & others to a very severe scrutiny of the style & grammar...& adding our first Journies and Visits to Scotland...It has given a gt. deal of trouble for one had so carefully to exclude even the slightest observation wh. might hurt any one's feelings, – but it has been an interest & an occupation – for no one can conceive the trouble of printing a book'.[19] She found it an immensely rewarding occupation, allowing her, as it did, to dwell happily and constructively on the past, while 'anxious to make it <u>as good</u> as possible, & that it shld. be read, especially by the <u>people</u> – her real friends. It shld. not be a <u>dear</u> book, so that <u>everyone</u> can buy it'.[20]

The publication on 10 January 1868 caused a sensation. 'From all & every side, high & low the feeling is the same & letters flow in – saying how much more than ever I shall be loved now that I am known & understood, & clamouring for a cheap edition for the poor – wh. will be ordered at once...It is very gratifying to see how people appreciate what is simple & right – & how especially my truest friends – the people feel it. They have (as a body) the truest feelings for family life'.[21] She felt that she was telling the upper classes how the lower classes should be treated: 'The kind & proper feeling towards the poor & the Servants will I hope do good for it is very much needed in England amongst the higher Classes'.[22] As she also wrote to the Crown Princess: 'The lower classes are becoming so well-informed, are so intelligent and earn their bread and riches so deservedly – that they cannot and ought not to be kept back – to be abused by the wretched, ignorant, high-born beings who love only to kill time'.[23] Lord Melbourne had regaled her in her youth with stories of the aristocracy and their behaviour, but since her marriage the Queen had had comparatively few friends among the 'upper 10,000' who, for the most part, neither understood nor appreciated her beloved Prince. She had a number of devoted friends and courtiers, but felt herself more in sympathy with the old women in the crofts on her estates in

85   *William Leighton Leitch*
Photograph in the Royal Library.

Aberdeenshire, than with the rich and frivolous world in which the Prince of Wales was moving.

The Queen always rejoiced in doing things that no other monarch had done and the *Leaves* was certainly a unique achievement. Through its pages the reader is 'drawn nearer to the every-day life of a living Queen than any persons not courtiers ever came before'.[24] Members of her household, however, were distressed by the footnotes, which gave the life histories of her gillies in exactly the same way as those of the aristocracy or her family. They were also embarrassed by her obvious bias in favour of her Highland servants.

In March 1868 the Queen made one of her rare visits to London to attend a Drawing Room. On her way back to the station, she had 'quite an ovation'. Carriages and crowds of people, three deep in places, greeted her and she felt it was largely due to the success of her book: 'It was very marked – especially as it was chiefly the so-called Upper 10,000 who are not near so loyal as the people. My book, every one says, has had such an extraordinary effect on the people'.[25]

That same month the 'People's edition' was published, at half a crown a copy, and sold in large quantities on both sides of the Atlantic. 20,000 copies were bespoken before publication and there had at once to be a reprint of 10,000. It is not surprising that the Queen was ecstatic. The nation's sympathy following the death of the Prince had largely evaporated, their monarch was seldom seen, so this literary success was enormously stimulating. The newspaper reviews were enthusiastic (or at least those shown to the Queen).

The cheap edition was followed by an elaborate illustrated one and with this the Queen was again closely involved. 'Evy. one likes to see what a place looks like',[26] she wrote with her practical good sense and set about selecting the plates. There were chromolithographs of the interiors of the sitting-rooms of the Queen and Prince, based on James Roberts's watercolours. There were full-page steel engravings, including Landseer's *Sunshine*, four of Haag's pictures and one of Wyld's. Finally, there was a series of vignettes, some taken from photographs, others from drawings by the royal couple and the rest based on watercolours. Most of these were drawn up by Edmund Wimperis and engraved by James Cooper. As several errors occur in the names of the artists in the list of plates, it is clear that they were never checked by the Queen herself.

In 1884 a further volume was published, *More Leaves from the Journal of a Life in the Highlands*, which continued the story from the death of the Prince Consort up to 1882. It was dedicated, not as the *Leaves* had been to the memory of 'him who made the life of the writer bright and happy', but to her 'Loyal Highlanders' and especially to 'my devoted personal attendant and faithful friend John Brown', who had recently died. A tribute to him concludes the book. Wise counsellors prevented

86 *John Brown* by George H. Thomas
Pencil, 32 × 23.7 cm, RL 14149

One of Thomas's studies, probably made for an oil painting of Brown leading the Queen's pony on a visit to the Mausoleum at Frogmore. This drawing was acquired by the Queen after the death of the artist.

the Queen from subsequently publishing a memoir of him, which would certainly have been misconstrued. In *More Leaves* most of the illustrations are based on photographs, but drawings by Nathaniel Green were used for three of them.

Another literary venture was to occupy the Queen from the mid-1860s. Joseph Noel Paton introduced her to the work of a fellow Scot, Kenneth MacLeay. MacLeay had made his reputation as a miniature painter but fell on hard times with the advent of photography, which virtually destroyed the market for miniatures. After commissioning MacLeay in 1864 to paint full-length watercolour portraits of her three youngest sons (89), the Queen ordered a series of her favourite

87 *Kenneth MacLeay*

A calotype by D.O. Hill and R. Adamson. Reproduced by kind permission of the Trustees of the National Portrait Gallery.

88 *John Brown* by Kenneth MacLeay

Watercolour, signed and dated 1866, 52·5 × 39·8 cm, RL 20711

'A good looking, tall lad of 23, with fair curly hair, so very good humoured & willing, – always ready to do whatever is asked, & always with a smile on his face' (Journal, 30 October 1850). He was a gillie at Balmoral from 1849 and in charge of the ponies there from 1855. Three years later the Queen appointed him her Personal Servant in Scotland, to wait upon her at all times, as she disliked having a change of attendants every week. At the end of 1864 Brown went south to be on duty at Osborne too and, in February 1865, he was appointed her Personal Servant wherever she was, not only in Scotland. She found him 'quite perfect, & with all the peculiar originality & shrewdness of his race'. She described him to the Crown Princess as 'so quiet, has such an excellent head and memory, and is besides so devoted, and attached and clever and so wonderfully able to interpret one's wishes'. This watercolour shows Brown against a background of Osborne House. It was reproduced as the second plate in MacLeay's *Highlanders*.

retainers at Balmoral (88, 91 and colour plate II on p18). After the *Leaves* had gone to press in 1865, she needed something new to occupy her mind. She planned, therefore, to extend the series of watercolour portraits to include representatives of all the most important Highland clans and to have them reproduced as chromolithographs. She embarked on the project with the support of the Dowager Duchess of Athole and her companion, Miss Amelia Murray MacGregor, an indomitable lady, cousin of the late Duke, who was to write the letterpress. MacLeay was sent all over Scotland to paint the clansmen and finally completed this assignment in 1869. The watercolours were exhibited in Bond Street that year and the book appeared in two handsome volumes during 1870. Unlike the plates in earlier books published on tartans and Highland dress, MacLeay's drawings depict actual clansmen, wearing whatever was considered to be the authentic clan tartan by their chieftain (92). He also illustrated any special clan trophies that had survived from the past. He contrived to give his sitters a distinction and an almost fashion-plate smartness that

Left
89   *Prince Arthur and Prince Leopold* by Kenneth MacLeay

Watercolour, signed and dated 1864, 32·2 × 22·7 cm, RL 14291

Right
90   *Arthur and Albert Grant* by Kenneth MacLeay

Watercolour, signed, 52·2 × 41·5 cm, RL 20744

The first of the Balmoral retainers to be painted by MacLeay, these sons of John Grant were at home, awaiting the arrival of the artist on 14 July 1865. MacLeay made them look as distinguished as the sons of the Queen in plate 89, but this would not have annoyed her.

Left
91 *John Grant* by Kenneth MacLeay

Watercolour, signed and dated 1865,
52·5 × 40·4 cm, RL 20710

A gillie to Sir Robert Gordon from 1832
and his Head Keeper from 1839. He was
kept on by the Queen and Prince,
becoming Head Forester and Keeper
until his retirement in 1875. Due to his
age, he was the one retainer permitted
to wear trousers, rather than the kilt.
This watercolour was reproduced as the
first plate in MacLeay's *Highlanders*.

Right
92 *Donald MacBeath and William Duff* by
Kenneth MacLeay

Watercolour heightened with white,
signed, 52·7 × 41·4 cm, RL 20720

The Atholemen chosen to represent their
clan in MacLeay's *Highlanders*. Both wear
Murray of Athole tartan.

appealed to the Queen. She thought there was no race like the Highlanders: 'these dear, good, superior, people wch. I miss dreadfully
elsewhere. Shrewd, clever, noble, vy. independent & proud in their
bearing – always answering you & speaking openly & strictly the truth,
with gt. <u>freedom</u>, but <u>ever</u> respectful'.[27] MacLeay produced just the
men the Queen wished to see.

On 27 December 1861 Carl Haag was visited in London by Franz
Winterhalter. He had just returned from Osborne, where he had been
summoned to paint a posthumous portrait of the Prince Consort. This
was the first of a whole series of portraits in every size and in every
medium commissioned by the Queen. Four days later Haag received a
request from her for a little book of sketches he had made at Balmoral
in 1853, which contained studies of the Prince. The Queen was collecting all the material she could find that recorded his appearance. In
May 1863 Haag was suddenly asked to go to Balmoral as soon as possible, to paint a picture of the Prince Consort. The Queen preferred to
have only one artist working for her at a time, wherever she was, and

93   *The Forest* by Carl Haag

Watercolour, 48·5 × 33·8 cm, RL 22060

The Prince returning from deer stalking. On the left, John Grant and another gillie with a pony, bearing a dead stag. On the right, James Morgan leading the pony Brechin.

had decided to invite Haag to Balmoral during her spring visit, as William and Richard Leitch were to be there in the autumn. When he received this summons, Haag went off to tell his friend Wilhelm Meyer, the Prince's Gentleman Rider, at the Royal Mews. The news was greeted with ribaldry, as Haag had sworn after his last visit that he would never work at Balmoral again; but now: 'What ten railway engines could not drag him to do, the Queen could achieve with one word!'

On his arrival at Balmoral on 28 May 1863, Carl Haag found himself lodged in the outbuildings, with a painting room in the castle itself. The Queen wished him to paint a small full-length portrait of the Prince in his shooting clothes, as if returning from stalking, followed by a servant leading his pony, with jägers, dogs and dead stags (93). Haag was provided with a plethora of photographs, busts and portraits in oil and watercolour to help him. He made a quick sketch for the composition and the Queen approved it.

The same afternoon Haag went up to Glen Gelder to sketch the landscape background for his picture. The Queen wished the watercolour to be finished by the time she left Scotland the following week, so there was no time to lose. She wrote to Princess Alice: 'I wanted some object so much, to occupy me, that I sent for good Carl Haag who arrived this Evg. & is to paint a Picture of darling Papa from Mr Corbould's Photo: in the Stalking dress! I saw him this Evg. & he seemed quite moved at being here after 10 years – & finding the new House – & – no blessed, beautiful, glorious & loving Master!'[28]

Queen Victoria followed each stage of Haag's work. On his return from Glen Gelder on that first evening, he was summoned to her and given stereoscopes of the glen with a photograph of the Prince touched up by the painter Horrack. The next morning Rudolf Löhlein, the Prince's valet, dressed in his master's clothes and sat to Haag as a model, while a bust was provided to help with the face. The Queen brought Prince Arthur to see Haag's work and suggested that as the young Prince was, of all her sons, the most like his father in colouring and complexion, Haag might also use him as a model.

On Haag's last day at Balmoral, after drawing John Grant (94), James Morgan and the deer-hounds, the Queen gave him a copy of the *Speeches and Addresses* of the Prince Consort, in which she had written so touching a dedication that the artist found it hard not to spend the afternoon in tears. In the evening she bade him farewell, showed him the death-mask of the Prince and expressed herself well satisfied with his 'really very striking painting'.[29] There was little light relief for Haag on this sombre visit, but he passed some evenings smoking oriental tobacco with Prince Alfred and exchanging stories about their travels. On one Sunday, he was also taken on an expedition up to Loch Muick and so feasted on chicken, ham, tarts, cheese, beer and whisky that he was unable to ride home, having to stop at Allt-na-giubhsaich to sleep it off for an hour before riding back to Balmoral.

The little picture known as *The Forest*, which the Queen felt had given Haag such 'a great deal of trouble',[30] was finished in London by 15 June. Two days later he took it down to Windsor Castle, where she instantly suggested some final alterations; he carried them out on the spot. Haag sent the finished watercolour to the Queen with a bill for 120 guineas: ten guineas a day for twelve days work. He was anxious to sell the copyright of the picture for a chromolithograph. He offered it first to Rowney and Co., who decided that it would be too difficult to reproduce the colours. Day and Son, however, agreed to take it on and

Haag was to receive eighty guineas for the copyright and six copies of the print. At the end of June Haag received a photograph of the picture from the Queen with a request that he should paint over it, as she could not bear to be without the picture for four months while it was being chromolithographed.

On 12 November Haag was summoned back to Windsor Castle. The Crown Princess was staying with her mother and considered that the figure of the Prince in the picture was too short and must be altered. When he saw the Queen, Haag committed the *faux pas* of telling her how well she looked. She told him sharply that appearances deceived and maintained that she not only felt ill but looked ill. Next day, pleased with Haag's alterations to the little watercolour, she ordered two more pictures from him, to be painted the following year.

Haag was in Germany when he received orders in May 1864 to return as soon as possible to execute the new commissions. He reached Balmoral on the afternoon of 25 May and was met by the Queen. She was eager that he should begin at once to make studies for some 'pictures of dear Memories'.[31] She now wanted three pictures to be completed in time for the next exhibition of the Society of Painters in Watercolour.

The first picture was to illustrate the 'Great Expedition' of 8-9 October 1861, when the royal party rode 129 miles to Glen Feshie and Blair. Having travelled sixty miles, they stayed at the small inn at Dalwhinnie, before driving on to Blair Castle. Escorted by the Duke of Athole, they drove up Glen Tilt to Forest Lodge, where they mounted ponies and rode up the glen, with the Duke's pipers playing the whole way before them. After an alfresco lunch ('I can't describe the beauty & wildness of the whole thing'[32]), the caravan moved on to the famous ford of the River Tarff. Following heavy rain the ford became almost impassable and, on this occasion, the water in the middle was nearly up to the men's waists. The painting was to show this scene – *The Fording of the Poll Tarff* (colour plate XX on p118). Beyond this point the path became even more precipitous and they rode on to the Bainoch. They had tea with Lady Fife before driving home by carriage to Balmoral, arriving after eight o'clock. Meanwhile the Duke's party had ridden back to Blair in the dark, each man with a handkerchief tied to his back, to guide the man behind him. They forded the Tarff two by two, arm in arm, singing 'God Save the Queen', with policemen's lanterns lit. The Duke got into his carriage at Forest Lodge, but it hit a bank and one horse broke his knee. The Duke completed the journey on foot. He reached home at one o'clock in the morning,[33] and would hardly have agreed with the Queen that 'this was the pleasantest & most enjoyable expedition I ever took'.[34]

Haag began work on *The Fording of the Poll Tarff* by making sketches of ten people and eight ponies at Balmoral. It was then arranged by the Dowager Duchess of Athole, whose husband had died of cancer the

XVIII *Balmoral, the Old and New Castles, Seen from the Opposite Side of the River Dee* by F. Colebrooke Stockdale

Watercolour with bodycolour, 31·3 × 47·2 cm, RL 19469

A rare view of both buildings before the final demolition of the old house in 1856. The Duchess of Kent owned watercolours by this artist of Abergeldie Castle and of the Saloon that she used on her visit to Brodick Castle in 1851. She may therefore have recommended his work to the Queen. He painted two views of Balmoral, for which he was paid twenty-five guineas in August 1856. He then went abroad with his brother.

XIX *Distant View of Allt-na-giubhsaich and Loch Muick* by Carlo Bossoli

Gouache, signed and dated 1856, 26·3 × 44 cm, RL 19508

The Italian artist, Carlo Bossoli, spent the three years preceding the Crimean War in attendance on Prince Woronzow, the Governor-General of New Russia, Bessarabia and the Crimea. In 1855 Bossoli brought to England over fifty landscape views of the countryside, which were of great public interest, as so little was known at home of the country where the war was being fought. The Queen met Bossoli and agreed to subscribe to his book of *Views in the Crimea*. In the following year, at Balmoral, the Prince bought this painting and the Queen a view of Ballater. Painted in a heavy gouache, they give a strikingly individual appearance to the familiar landscape.

XVIII

XIX

Above
XX   *The Fording of the Poll Tarff* by Carl Haag

Watercolour with scraping out, signed and dated 1865, 63·3 × 127 cm, RL 22001

The cortège is led by the guide Charles Stewart, followed by the pipers Eneas Rose and Jock McPherson. McPherson had been Pipe-Major at the Eglinton Tournament in 1839 and was succeeded by Rose as piper to the Duke of Athole. The Duke of Athole is seen wading through the ford, leading the Queen's horse, with John Brown on her right and Sandy McAra, the Duke's Head Forester, on her left. Behind the Queen rides the Prince Consort and beside him Princess Alice, whose horse is led by Donald MacBeath. Prince Louis of Hesse comes next, with James Morgan up behind him. In the foreground General Grey is up in front of Peter Robertson. Jock McAra

leads the horse of Lady Churchill; John Grant and J. Smith ride one pony down the hill on the left, followed by five more of the Duke's men.

Reviewed in the *Art Journal* (1865, p173), the picture was criticised for things that had also worried Haag: 'the weight of the background somewhat over-powers the rest of the picture, and the exclusion of the blue heavens denies variety to the insuperable monotony of colour. The figures are most carefully painted, and the equanimity which the whole group maintains under circumstances not a little agitating, is subject to admiration. Could even the smallest accident have been permitted, it would have helped the artist amazingly through the tedium of his task. The peat-brown hue of the mountain stream unfortunately takes from the painter his last chance of getting into his colours cool grey and compensating blue. The picture is chiefly of personal interest, and as such it will be prized'.

Opposite, above
XXI   *A View of Carn Lochan, Looking towards Perth* by Richard P. Leitch

Watercolour with bodycolour, signed and dated 1862, 21 × 41 cm, RL 19685

The setting for the picnic luncheon on 16 October 1861, which was also drawn by Haag. The Prince is shown leading the Queen's pony and pointing out the view, 'where one can look right up the valley for an immense distance'.

Opposite, below
XXII   *Luncheon at Carn Lochan* by Carl Haag

Watercolour, signed and dated 1865, 34 × 49·4 cm, RL 22058

The Queen and Prince are shown on the right with Princess Helena. This was the only expedition in which the Princess took part. The engaged couple, Princess Alice and Prince Louis of Hesse, are seated on the left. John Grant and John Brown are in attendance.

XXI

XXII

XXIII

XXIV

XXIII *Loch Muick, with the Shiel of the Glasallt* by William Wyld

Watercolour and bodycolour heightened with white, signed, 22·3 × 33·7 cm, RL 19555

A view painted in 1852 of the shiel, which had been built the previous year for the keeper, Charles Duncan. The Queen described it as a 'truly sylvan abode', but the keeper's wife found it 'dreadfully remote'.

XXIV *The Glasallt Shiel* by William Simpson

Watercolour, signed and dated 1882, 22·7 × 35 cm, RL 23188

The Queen is shown with John Brown at the door of the house. The ladies sketching in the boat are probably the Duchess of Edinburgh and the Duchess of Connaught, who visited the shiel with the Queen on 13 September 1881. At that time, Simpson was staying at Abergeldie and taken up to the Glasallt. He was paid twenty guineas for this watercolour and the one of the Garden Cottage (106).

previous January, that Haag should go to Blair to sketch the Athole retainers for the picture. After a journey in torrential rain, partly on horseback and partly by dog-cart, Haag set up his studio in the entrance hall at Blair Castle. The Dowager Duchess had moved out after her husband's death and the new Duke was in Canada. The castle had been let, but the tenants had not moved in and Haag was given a friendly welcome by the Athole retainers. They were delighted with his portraits of them (95) and finally the weather improved enough for him to sketch the falls of the Tarff, before returning south on 17 June. Next he went to Windsor Castle to draw the Prince and Princess of Hesse. Princess Alice, who had married Prince Louis of Hesse in July 1862, was expecting her second child, so she did not wish to sit on a saddle. Haag had to paint her figure from photographs and only the head from life. He found her a difficult model, as she moved endlessly and played with her daughter, but he had more success next day when he worked from a photograph, before having an hour-long sitting with the Princess.

After an autumn on the Continent, Haag began the large-scale painting in mid-December. The Queen returned his sketches and he drew out his cartoon, laying in the figures and ponies, while building up the tones of the composition with stump. On 7 January 1865 he stretched the paper for the final picture and laid in the outlines, followed by the coloured tones. A week later he began to transfer the figures to the paper. A month later he had transferred all the figures and the ponies, but was depressed by his waterfall background. He found it too dark in tone and too flat, despite attempts to lighten it by removing the paint with a wash leather. Fellow artists like Thomas M. Richardson, Henry Hine and the Fripp brothers offered advice, but Haag seemed unable to complete the picture as he wished.

Towards the end of February he took it to Windsor, where the Queen gave him five sittings, even wearing her costume and sitting for him in the saddle. All through March he worried about his painting, despairing of ever completing it for the exhibition. Finally he achieved the effect he wanted, by lightening the cliffs in the background to left and right, thereby setting back the central waterfall and pulling the whole composition together. He added clouds of mist rising over the water, strengthened the reflections in the foreground and was satisfied at last. He now needed only to complete the figure of the Prince Consort. Back at Windsor he was told to use Prince Alfred ('grown & so like his dear Father') as a model, but had more success working from memory. Haag covered his picture with his own wax solution, and set it into a frame he had designed himself, made by Foord and Dickinson. The painting was finally ready just in time for exhibition at the Society of Painters in Watercolour.

Much relieved, Haag went off to Oberwesel to visit the medieval 'Red Tower' that he was restoring as a house and studio. While he was

away, Landseer went to Osborne and was commissioned to illustrate two subjects, which later became known as *Sunshine* and *Shadow*. The second of these was to show the Queen on a pony accompanied by the younger Princesses. This was the other subject outlined to Haag at the end of 1863. When Haag returned to Balmoral on 22 May, he did not know why his instructions had been altered, but he was now told to paint a scene in the Corrie Buie (or Choire Bhuidhe), a favourite hillside on the edge of the Ballochbuie forest (96). It was to be a 'pretty Pendant to dear Papa's picture...I sitting – Lenchen at my feet – & Louise standing behind me – Grant & Brown in the distance waiting for us – with a Plaid, drawing books &c'.[35] As Haag sat in pouring rain attempting to envisage and draw a spring evening, the Queen arrived to take tea on the hillside with Princess Helena and the Dowager Duchess of Athole; they sent a cup across to the artist.

On 24 May Haag drew the group of figures on the scale of the final picture. He was given sittings by all the royal ladies, as well as by John Grant and John Brown. The Queen was highly amused by Brown's

Opposite, left
94   *John Grant* by Carl Haag

Pencil and wash, dated 4 June 1863,
12·7 × 17·7 cm, RL 21318 f 12

Detail of a study for *The Forest* (93).

Opposite, right
95   *Jock McAra* by Carl Haag

Watercolour, dated 14 June 1864,
24·1 × 16·8 cm
Reproduced by kind permission of the
Duke of Atholl

A study for *The Fording of the Poll Tarff*.
During his week at Blair, Haag drew the
falls, a pony and eight of the Duke of
Athole's retainers. He thought this
drawing of the hillman was the best of the
group, but in the finished painting, where
McAra leads Lady Churchill's pony, only
his head is visible. When Haag left Blair,
McAra delighted him by saying that he
was the pleasantest gentleman he had
ever met; if only he could have spoken
Gaelic, he would have been perfect. 'I am
sorry you are ganging awa fro us and hope
ye will come agin for me to see ye'. All the
studies of the Duke's men are at Blair
Castle, but the posthumous portrait of the
Duke himself cannot be traced.

comment: 'I hate sitting to an Artist, for I see no use in it; I should not
object so much if a body could be benefited by this stupid Art of
painting'. Princess Helena stood or knelt endlessly for him. On one
occasion, she posed for three hours in an exhausting position and
nearly fainted when she moved. Fräulein Singer, one of the Queen's
dressers, posed in the Queen's clothes and grumbled the whole time,
complaining of headaches, nerves and cold feet, until he told her of

96   *Corrie Buie* by Carl Haag

Watercolour, signed and dated 1865,
51 × 35.5 cm, RL 17111

The Queen seated in the heather, with
Princess Helena at her knee. Princess
Louise stands behind, to the left. John
Brown and John Grant approach on the
right.

the patience of the Princess. No doubt even sitting to Haag helped to relieve the tedium of the long days at Balmoral; the artist had to force Princess Helena to rest from their sittings. He found her full of intelligence, energy and kindness, while her sister was charming, serious and calm.

Haag's third and final work for the Queen was to show *The Luncheon of the Royal Family at Carn Lochan*, a subject she was very anxious to have, as it had been the climax of the last expedition, on 16 October 1861, with Prince Louis of Hesse, Princess Alice and Princess Helena (colour plate XXII on p119). They had gone up above Loch Callater and lunched at a precipitous spot above the valley of Carn Lochan (or Caen Lochan) with the River Isla winding through it far below, before descending again to the Spittal Bridge. Richard Leitch had already made small watercolours of both this subject and the fording of the Tarff, but the Queen obviously felt that Haag would be better able to do justice to subjects so near to her heart. She liked his first scheme for the *Luncheon* picture and thought it promised to be very successful.

Carl Haag went back to London from Balmoral exhausted and un-able to work. The Queen told him to do no more to the picture until the autumn and, much relieved, he set off again to Oberwesel. There he fired mortars and illuminated his Tower with a red glow in honour of the Queen as she passed twice through the station at Oberwesel on her journeys to Darmstadt and Coburg, in August and September. Haag stood bowing on his balcony, but probably his old mother was the only person to appreciate this display of loyalty.

Back in London by early November 1865, Haag completed the *Corrie Buie* picture and began work on *Luncheon at Carn Lochan*. The Queen gave him a short sitting at Windsor, but he had to paint the other likenesses from memory and found this a tedious and thankless task. He took the picture down to Windsor on 15 December, but the Queen's uncle Leopold had just died and she could not see the artist. Instead, she sent for the picture several times and issued instructions for alterations, which Haag carried out, until she finally announced herself satisfied.

The story of the Queen's patronage of Haag closes on rather an ugly note. By the end of 1865, he was depressed with his last commission and anxious about his finances. It was not until 22 December that he received a cheque for £829.5s.6d to cover the three watercolours he had painted for the Queen over the last eighteen months. He had received little income from other sources during that time. In August 1864 he had been paid 250 guineas, at a rate of ten guineas a day for twenty-five days work, while making his studies for the *Poll Tarff* pic-ture at Balmoral and Blair Castle. The Queen thought these charges excessive and vowed never to employ him again. Other artists who worked for her, like Keyl and Burton Barber, only charged three guineas a day for their time. If Haag had known that he would never again be employed by the Queen he might not have minded greatly, although her commissions had helped to make his name and his work for her had been well received at exhibitions.

In 1868 the Queen wished to use engravings from four of Haag's paintings as plates in the illustrated edition of her *Leaves from the Journal of Our Life in the Highlands*. Haag considered that he had been underpaid in 1854 for his two large pictures of *Morning* and *Evening at Balmoral*. Sir Charles Phipps had assured him that he could keep the copyright of the pictures for himself, have the pictures engraved and thus make more money. He now found that he was expected to give his copyright away gratis, by allowing the reproduction of his paintings in the Queen's book. He was furious and said that in this case he should have been paid £560 more when he had painted the pictures. He reckoned he should now be given £560 for the copyright, plus interest at three per cent. The Queen was equally angry and complained to Theodore Martin, her chosen author for the *Life of the Prince Consort*, that she feared Carl Haag might be found troublesome as he was so very greedy. Haag finally agreed to accept £200, in return for his permission to reproduce the paintings on this one occasion only. He was told that he could keep the copyright himself for any other purpose. In July 1868 Queen Victoria wrote to Martin that she was most grateful to him for all the trouble he had taken about 'this very tiresome Carl Haag whom she is <u>really</u> ashamed of, – & will certainly <u>not</u> employ again'.[36] Nevertheless the Queen was very proud of the paintings that he had done for her and frequently allowed them to be exhibited, although on principle she disliked lending pictures to exhibitions.[37]

97 *The Royal Family taking Luncheon on the Top of Lochnagar* by Carl Haag

Pencil with sepia wash, 12·7 × 17·7 cm, RL 21318 f3

This sketch, made in his notebook in 1853, may have helped Haag to recall a royal picnic when he was commissioned to reconstruct the luncheon on Carn Lochan (colour plate XXII on p119).

98 *Sunshine, or the Death of the Royal Stag* by Sir Edwin Landseer

Pastel and chalks, 85 × 110.5 cm, RL 22020

The Prince with his deerhounds and John Grant with the dead stag. The Queen is riding up, on a pony led by John Brown.

A happier postscript completes the story. When Haag made his final appearance at Windsor on 8 July 1899, bringing his *Golden Gate of the Temple at Jerusalem* to show her, she wrote in her Journal: 'I knew him very well formerly, having had lessons with him & possess many fine pictures by him…He is very much altered & seemed quite overcome at seeing me'.[38]

After his visit to Balmoral in September 1853, Sir Edwin Landseer did not return to paint there for fourteen years. However, he was invited to Osborne in May 1865. There he drew, in four days, a large pastel of Princess Beatrice on her pony. It was a subject that had been discussed the previous year, but postponed because of Landseer's constant illness. The Queen found him in good spirits. He was her only

Left
99 *The Prince Consort and Queen Victoria*

A photograph taken by John Mayall on
1 March 1861 and coloured by
E.H. Corbould. On the Queen's orders, a
number of artists used this photograph to
try and recapture the appearance of the
Prince (see plates 98 and 100).

Right
100 *The Prince Consort* by Kenneth
MacLeay

Watercolour, signed and dated 1866,
52·2 × 32 cm, RL 14290

With the keeper Charles Duncan and
Lochnagar in the distance.

guest at the time. Lady Ponsonby, the wife of the Private Secretary,
described how very pleasant he made himself, while the Queen 'in
high force, talked all dinner time, and [was] highly amused at Landseer's anecdotes, about his animals etc'.[39]

He seemed to be in such good form that the Queen was 'seized with
a great wish that he should do 2 more chalk sketches, the one rep-
resenting dearest Albert with a stag that he had shot, at his feet, & I
coming up in the distance, with one of the Children to look at it.
Then, the reverse of that bright happy time, I, as I am now, sad &
lonely, seated on my pony, led by Brown, with a representation of
Osborne & a dedication telling the present sad truth. Sir E. Landseer is
delighted at the idea & most ready to do it'.[40] The two pictures were
to become known as *Sunshine*, or the *Death of the Royal Stag with the
Queen Riding up to Congratulate His Royal Highness* (98), and *Shadow*,
or *Her Majesty at Osborne in 1866*.

Before leaving Osborne, Landseer showed the Queen his first ideas for the pictures and a week after his departure he was ready to show her his designs for the new subjects, with their contrasting moods of 'Sunny Days and Dark Ones',[41] as she expressed it. Problems arose, as always, with work that Landseer could not carry out at once. He hoped he would have 'healthy work enough' in him to realise her expectations. He then found he could not obtain the vellum he needed; the Queen decided that she wanted drawings made twice the size of the original sketches for private lithographs she was planning. Two years after beginning, the pictures were still incomplete and Landseer was trying to improve his likeness of the Prince. As the basis for his portrait, he was expected to use, as MacLeay and Corbould had done, the photograph taken by John Mayall in March 1861 (99). The Prince's shooting clothes were doubtless made available to Landseer, as they had been to Haag. The composition was perhaps consciously reminiscent

101 *Death of the Stag in Glen Tilt* by Sir Edwin Landseer

Oil on canvas, 149·8 × 200·8 cm Reproduced by kind permission of the Duke of Atholl

The 4th Duke of Atholl with his grandson, George Murray (later Lord Glenlyon and then 6th Duke of Athole) with keepers. This seminal work in Landseer's *oeuvre* was exhibited at the Royal Academy in 1830.

102 *Brechin* by Sir Edwin Landseer

Pastel, 52·8 × 75 cm, RL 22014

The shooting pony ridden by the Prince from 1859 to October 1861, with a gillie and dead ptarmigan. After the death of the Prince, the Queen and Princess Alice occasionally rode Brechin: 'his own pony, which is so precious to me, he having always ridden him' (Journal); see plate 93.

of one of Landseer's earliest large Scottish subjects, the *Death of the Stag in Glen Tilt*, painted for the 4th Duke of Atholl in 1829 (101) The Queen probably remembered it from her first visit to Blair Castle in 1844.

The Queen was very loyal to Landseer. She invited him to stay at Balmoral in 1867, for what proved to be his last visit. He wrote thanking her for the 'highly flattering invitation and truly gracious proposal that I should revive my eyes and health by the comforting breezes of Balmoral'.[42] He seems to have managed to complete and dispatch both chalk drawings to precede him there on 21 May. Although she already had several pictures of the Prince Consort's old shooting pony, Brechin, the Queen wanted Landseer to draw her another. He wrote on 14 May that he had never made any sketches of the pony, but when he visited Balmoral at the end of the month he completed a large pastel of Brechin within a few days (102). While staying at the castle Landseer

wrote home to Jessie, his sister and housekeeper, saying that he felt wretchedly weak and had had no appetite since his arrival in the Highlands. Drawing tired him, there was unceasing cold rain and he could not get out of doors: 'Flogging would be mild compared to my sufferings. No sleep, fearful cramp at night, accompanied by a feeling of faintness and distressful feebleness'.[43] The Queen, oblivious of his sufferings, told the Crown Princess that he was 'doing some beautiful things, and I never saw him more amiable or more *en train* and amenable to observation'.[44]

When the Queen saw Landseer at a garden party at Chiswick in 1871, she was distressed by his appearance. On his death two years later, she wrote of the merciful release of this 'great artist & kind old friend', who had for the last three years been 'in a most distressing state, half out of his mind, yet not entirely so'.[45]

103 *Young Noble and Bess* by Gourlay Steell

Chalk, watercolour, bodycolour and pastel, signed and dated 1884, 37·5 × 52 cm, RL 23092

Gourlay Steell succeeded Landseer as Animal Painter for Scotland and continued the series of animal portraits that the Queen liked to keep for her records, even though she also had many photographs of her dogs. This drawing was made at Windsor and hung in the kennels there.

Chapter Seven

The Last Years

At Balmoral the Queen could escape from the formality of her life in the south and sometimes liked to retreat to a still more remote spot, the small hut, Allt-na-giubhsaich, 'our wild little place near Loch Muick'. In 1848 the Queen and Prince had a cold luncheon in one of the rooms there. After this they decided to build on to the shiel, so that they could stay the night with few attendants and enjoy its remoteness. By August 1849 the transformation was complete. Two wooden huts had been added (104, 105) and now they had 'a charming little dining-room, sitting-room, bed-room and dressing-room, all _en suite_'.[1] There was a room for the Maid of Honour and for the lady's maid, and a little pantry. The kitchen and staff rooms were in huts behind. The Queen and Prince paid many visits to the shiel. They loved to walk round the little garden after dinner: 'the silence and solitude, only interrupted by the waving of the fir trees, were very solemn and striking'.[2]

After the death of the Prince Consort, the shiel became the property of the Prince of Wales. The Queen could not bear to stay there again, but she sometimes took tea there and it soothed her to find that everything was 'as we left it, speaking of happy days in the past'.[3] Now she needed once more 'some _little_ Spot' to go to occasionally for a night or two of quiet and seclusion, 'to _rest_ from the never ceasing interruptions & work wh. she has to endure every day of her sad & desolate life'.[4] She already had a room she could use for an occasional meal in the Glasallt Shiel, another keeper's lodge, at the west end of Loch Muick (colour plate XXIII on p120). The obvious plan was to extend this house, especially as the Prince, who had described it as 'quite a Dwelling' for the 'Lady of the Lake',[5] had himself thought of building there

and planned some alterations. The additions were discussed in 1866 and on 1 October 1868 the Queen slept there, in her '1st widow's house – not blessed by him'.[6] She often stayed thereafter, guarded only by her faithful Highlanders and, at night, by one policeman (colour plate XXIV on p120). Sir Henry Ponsonby felt that she always returned 'much the better and livelier' for her visits to the shiel, although he would not himself have chosen so lonely a spot.[7] On 29 March 1883 John Brown died. The Glasallt was 'now most terrible for her to visit – it is like <u>death</u>, <u>far</u> more than the peaceful Kirkyard…The <u>Queen</u> can never <u>live</u> at the Glasallt <u>again</u>. The whole thing was planned & arranged by him. He meant everything there. <u>That</u> bright Chapter in her saddened life is closed <u>for ever</u>!'[8] Although she occasionally visited the Glasallt for a meal, the Queen never again stayed there, preferring to use the Danzig Shiel, which had been completed for her in 1882.

In 1881 William Simpson went north to paint a series of watercolours of Balmoral and surrounding places, which give a most attractive

105 *Allt-na-giubhsaich, Prince Albert's Dressing-room* by George M.Greig

Watercolour heightened with white, 26·4 × 36·8 cm, RL 19501

In 1862 and early 1863 Greig painted interiors of the royal suite at the Palace of Holyroodhouse, used briefly each autumn from 1850 until 1861. In the autumn of 1863, Greig drew the rooms at the country inns where the royal couple had stayed on their 'Great Expeditions'. He also painted interiors of Allt-na-giubhsaich, of which only one can now be traced. It illustrates the simple style in which the Queen and Prince lived. 'Our rooms are delightfully papered, ceilings as well as walls, and very nicely furnished'. The Prince's evening clothes are shown laid out as if he were about to change for dinner.

view of the Queen's surroundings during her widowhood. 'Crimean Simpson' had worked intermittently for her since the outbreak of the Crimean War, when she had allowed him to dedicate to her his book *The Seat of War in the East*. As Special Artist to the *Illustrated London News*, he recorded the Prince of Wales's tour of India in 1875-76. In 1881 Simpson was asked to make sketches for a series of views of 'English Homes' to be published in the *Illustrated London News*. He went up to Balmoral in August, with orders to make his drawings before the arrival of the Queen (106). He visited Edinburgh to record the Volunteer Review, which took place on 25 August, and then returned north on 10 September to stay with the Prince of Wales at Abergeldie. The completed watercolours are dated 1882, so Simpson must have finished them later from sketches made on the spot.[9]

Among the paintings are views of both the exterior and interior of the old church at Crathie (107, 108). It had been built in the first years of the nineteenth century in a simple style, but the arrival of the royal family in the late 1840s put a considerable strain on its space.

106 *The Garden Cottage at Balmoral* by William Simpson

Watercolour, signed and dated 1882, 22·2 × 32·7 cm, RL 23187

The Queen frequently had breakfast on the verandah and sat there for 'writing or signing', as she can be seen doing in Simpson's watercolour. When it was reproduced in the *Illustrated London News*, the figure of the Queen was omitted and a Highland servant was inserted, carrying her umbrella, plaid and book.

107 *Crathie, the Old Church* by William Simpson

Watercolour, with bodycolour, signed and dated 1882, 23 × 33 cm, RL 19534

108 *Crathie, the Interior of the Old Church* by William Simpson

Watercolour, signed and dated 1882, 29·8 × 44 cm, RL 19535

On the preacher's left can be seen the Queen, with two of her daughters-in-law, Prince Leopold and Princess Beatrice. The Prince of Wales sits with his family in the Abergeldie pew in front of the preacher. By this date the Queen seldom attended the kirk, preferring to have services held for her in the castle.

109 *William Simpson*

Photograph reproduced by kind permission of Mr B. Howarth-Loomes

The Queen gave great pleasure to her Scottish subjects by attending the services of the Church of Scotland and thereby bridging the gulf 'torn open by the madness of Laud and Charles I'. She 'rebuked, by silent acts, which are more powerful than words, the un-wisdom of those members of the Scotch aristocracy, who, looking down upon the Kirk as vulgar and democratic…have deserted it for the Scotch Episcopal Church, or even for the communion of Rome' thus causing 'a breach

110 *Laying the Foundation Stone of the New Church at Crathie on 11 September 1893* by John Mitchell

Watercolour, signed and dated 1893, 37·8 × 54·5 cm, RL 22002

The Queen laid the foundation stone, then three of her granddaughters, Princess Margaret and Princess Victoria Patricia of Connaught with Princess Victoria Eugenie of Battenberg laid corn, wine and oil upon it. John Mitchell was an Aberdeen painter and his watercolour was used as an illustration in *Under Lochnagar* (1894), a book edited by the factor, Dr Profeit, and sold to raise money for the rebuilding of the church.

111 *Crathie, the New Church from the Old Road* by John Mitchell

Watercolour, signed and dated 1897, 37·5 × 54·3 cm, RL 22003

When the new church was being planned, the Queen's daughters were full of suggestions. Princess Beatrice wanted a tower, like one of the gates at Coburg, imposed upon a Gothic building. Princess Louise considered that her sister knew nothing of architecture and 'sketched out something which bowled over Pss B's German sort of cupola. Her design won the day'. The architect A.Marshall Mackenzie of Edinburgh was employed. The church was completed in 1895.

between themselves and their own tenantry'.[10] From November 1873 the Queen took communion at Crathie Church each autumn. In November 1893 the old building was demolished; although the Queen thought it 'certainly very ugly', she had grown fond of it and was sad to visit it for the last time. She laid the foundation stone of the new church in September 1893, when the walls were already three or four feet high (110, 111).

112 *The Meeting before the Deer Drive in Abergeldie Wood* by Count Mihály Zichy

Pencil with ink and sepia and grey wash, 73 × 52.2 cm, RL 22063

The Prince of Wales, with the Duke of Edinburgh walking beside him, greets Prince Louis of Hesse, who was staying at Balmoral with Princess Alice and their children in September 1871 when this drawing was made.

When he was staying at Abergeldie, the Prince of Wales occasion-ally attended services at Crathie Church with his mother; but relations between them were not easy. After the death of the Prince Consort, the Queen exercised complete control over the shooting on the entire estate and the Prince of Wales was not even allowed to organise the shooting at Abergeldie without his mother's permission. He was a keen shot and he invited the Hungarian painter Count Mihály Zichy, who

113 *Bringing Home the Dead Stag* by Count Mihály Zichy

Sepia ink with grey, white, blue and sepia wash, signed and dated 1872, 65 × 82 cm, RL 22026

114 *On the Way to the Stalk* by Count Mihály Zichy

Pencil, ink and sepia wash, signed, 37·8 × 53 cm, RL 22028

The Prince of Wales rides ahead, with Donald Stewart beside him. Captain Arthur Ellis follows on horseback.

had worked at the Imperial Russian court for twenty-five years, to visit Abergeldie on several occasions in the 1870s. Working mainly in ink with sepia and grey washes, Zichy produced an evocative series of seventeen drawings, which complement the watercolours that Haag had made for the Queen (112-115).

115   *Luncheon out Stalking on Lochnagar*
by Count Mihály Zichy

Pencil, sepia ink and grey and sepia wash,
signed and dated 1872, 34·7 × 25·5 cm,
RL 22024

The Prince of Wales eating sandwiches
with the artist.

In October 1881 the Queen saw the work of the painter Nathaniel
Everett Green, who 'sketches most beautifully, & comes nearly every
year to Scotland'.[11] She found him an amusing and admirable teacher.
She drew beside him and liked his way of saying things 'so funnily &
pompously'.[12] She bought many of his watercolours (116), chiefly to
give away as presents. He also gave lessons to Princess Beatrice.

While taking tea at the Danzig Shiel in June 1895, the Queen 'saw
there some beautiful sketches by an artist of the name of Ottewell,
who has spent several months in Braemar, painting, having been

Amadée Forestier, who had covered the Queen's stay in Florence for the *Illustrated London News* in 1893 was also at Balmoral. After the visit, Forestier sent up his sketchbook of drawings and suggested that he should work up three of them for the Queen. She only wanted the scene of the reception of the guests, however, and when this was delivered it elicited a sharp memorandum: the Emperor should be made more prominent, the Indian servant was too tall. The drawing was duly altered (120), but the Queen still did not 'care about it'.[18] The problems that had confronted a painter in the 1840s still faced her artists fifty years later.

The sadness of the Queen's last visit to Balmoral in the late autumn of 1900 is summed up by Marie Mallet, one of her Extra Women of the Bedchamber: 'The dear little Queen makes heroic efforts to be cheerful but her face in repose is terribly sad...The curious thing is that she said to me, "After the Prince Consort's death I wished to die, but now I wish to live and do what I can for my country and those I love"...She was a little brighter yesterday, but still ate so little. I could kill the cooks who take no pains whatever to prepare tempting little dishes and would be a disgrace to any kitchen. How I should like to work a sweeping reform, we are abominably served just now. The footmen smell of whisky and are never prompt to answer the bell and although they do not speak rudely, they stare in such a supercilious way. As for the Queen's dinner it is more like a badly arranged picnic'.[19]

The Queen's eldest daughter was mortally ill with cancer, and her second son, Alfred, who had succeeded his uncle as Duke of Saxe-Coburg-Gotha in 1893, had died in August: 'this terrible blow fell like

Opposite, left

119 *The Imperial Party Arriving at Balmoral on 22 September 1896* by Orlando Norie
Watercolour heightened with white, signed, 45·3 × 98·4 cm, RL 23604

Although the evening was cold and wet, the Emperor and Empress left Ballater Station and arrived at the castle with the carriages open, to be greeted by assembled pipers. The Queen's Highlanders escorted the procession from Dee Bridge, bearing lighted torches. They drove with the Prince of Wales, who wore the uniform of the Kiev 27th Imperial Dragoons. The Emperor was wearing the uniform of the Scots Greys. He had been made Honorary Colonel of the Scots Greys by Queen Victoria as a wedding present and they formed the mounted escort on this occasion. Bonfires were lit on all the surrounding hills and church bells were rung.

120 *The Queen Greeting the Emperor and Empress of Russia at Balmoral* by Amadée Forestier

Watercolour, signed and dated 1896, 22·4 × 31·5 cm, RL 23195

The most prominent figures, from left to right, are Princess Margaret of Connaught, the Duchess of Connaught, Princes Alexander, Maurice and Leopold of Battenberg, the Prince of Wales, the Empress, Queen Victoria, the Emperor, the Grand Duchess Olga, the Duke of Connaught and the Duke of York.

a clap of thunder, taking again a beloved grown up Child – the 3rd from me!'[20] Out driving at Balmoral, she passed blocks of granite from a local quarry on their way to Aberdeen for the Duke's tomb: 'I thought he would have liked the idea, of its coming from Balmoral itself, but it gave me quite a turn seeing it, & knowing what use it was going to be put to'.[21] One day she took tea at Allt-na-giubhsaich, which she had not done for a long time. 'Tea' now consisted only of arrowroot with milk. She had not been feeling well for the last few days and could eat very little. She was kept in constant touch with the events of the Boer War ('always fresh lives lost'[22]). Another terrible blow was the death of a favourite grandson, 'Christle', Prince Christian Victor of Schleswig-Holstein, who died of enteric fever on the eve of his return from South Africa.

On her last day at Balmoral, after calling at Donald Stewart's house to wish his family goodbye and to give him a photogravure of 'dear Affie', the Queen lunched in Prince Albert's room with Princess Beatrice and her children. As she drove away from the Castle, the day was 'wretchedly gloomy & dark'.[23] She did not realise that it was her failing sight, as well as the weather, that was blurring the familiar landscape. With her, the Queen carried a wreath to lay on Prince Albert's tomb in the Mausoleum at Frogmore, where within three months she was to join him, her long widowhood over at last.

Left
121   *Queen Victoria* by Josefine Swoboda

Watercolour, signed, 45·6 × 35·4 cm, oval, RL 21637

Josefine Swoboda, sister of the Viennese oil painter Rudolf Swoboda, came to England in the 1890s and made a number of watercolour portraits for Queen Victoria. She drew the Queen at Balmoral in May 1893. After three sittings, the Queen thought the picture was 'getting very like' and when it was completed on 5 June she found it 'very successful'.

Right
122   *Anne, Dowager Duchess of Athole* by Josefine Swoboda

Watercolour, signed and dated 1893, 43·6 × 34 cm, oval, RL 17116

A lifelong friend of the Queen, the Duchess had been her hostess at Blair Castle in 1844. She was Mistress of the Robes, 1852-53, and Lady of the Bedchamber, 1854-97. She was instrumental in carrying out the project of MacLeay's *Highlanders*.

Appendix

Carl Haag's Technique

The reviews of Haag's exhibited watercolours show that his technique intrigued contemporary critics; the methods he used are described in his diaries. As an art student in Nuremberg, Carl Haag painted in oils, but he was always interested in watercolour and made small portraits in that medium when he moved to Munich. On his arrival in London in 1847, he began to study English watercolour technique, as against the more opaque gouache methods practised on the Continent. Haag decided to use oils for his studies, to obtain the desired depth of local colour quickly, and then to carry out his finished paintings for exhibition in watercolour, in order to achieve a greater clarity and naturalism.

To test the durability of the watercolour pigments, at that time much in question, Haag carried out various experiments assisted by Frederick Abel, who later became an eminent chemist. They proved that the mineral-based colours withstood exposure to light, while the vegetable pigments were much more transient. An accident with an exploding powder-bottle, which nearly cost Haag the use of his right hand, meant that he could spend the many hours of convalescence considering his new techniques. He abandoned the meticulous miniature-like style in which he had previously painted portraits, evolving a method of putting on his colour very strongly and then gradually removing it again. In 1850 his first watercolours were exhibited at the Society of Painters in Watercolour, where he had recently been elected an Associate. They were not well received by the critic of *The Athenaeum*,[1] but were liked by others. Three years later the reviewer in *The Athenaeum* wrote of Haag's *Marino Faliero and the Spy* that he 'exhibits a totally different manner of treating watercolours, with a

123 *Carl Haag*

A photograph taken in August 1863 by Cundall Downes & Co.
Reproduced by kind permission of Mrs P. Allison

force which approaches corruption. For corrupt we must hold to be such use of body-colour as gives to the picture the husky air of a crayon-drawing'.[2] The reviewer in the *Illustrated London News* thought that, 'as a specimen of colouring', his *Marino Faliero* 'is one of the richest and most harmonious we have ever met with in this medium'.[3]

Haag never used opaque white in his watercolours. He did not trust its permanence when used with other pigments, although he thought it a permanent pigment in itself. To achieve white highlights he always scraped out the paint.

When he was painting life studies in Rome during the winter of 1852, Haag carefully noted the method in his diary and it is similar to the one he was to use for his studies at Balmoral the following autumn. He describes how he tinted his paper with grey ink, by first putting one layer of yellow, then of red, then painting it all over in blue, brushing the whole over together with a large bristle brush to give a light, mottled grey. He would then lay in his figure with a few strokes of charcoal, to get the proportions. Next he built up the shadows and modelled the form, using burnt umber for the face, hands and other parts of the flesh. He used vandyke brown for the shadowed folds of the costume and a strong yellow-grey for the white parts. Haag painted the highlights with water only, to soften the paint on the area, then mopped the colour off with blotting paper and, in some cases, with india rubber. Thereby, he either achieved a grey half-tone or got back to the original white paper. Having established the tones he required, Haag set about applying his local colour.

The Queen frequently borrowed drawings by Haag to copy and she made very passable versions of his figure studies, apparently using his techniques. Only in one of her landscape paintings, an ambitious study of a mountain range,[4] does she seem to have used his method of scraping away the paint to get back to the white paper, so giving the effect of snow and highlights. Perhaps Haag helped her on this occasion. She seems not to have repeated the experiment, but returned to her usual method of adding imposed whites.

Haag also invented a special fixative for his finished watercolours, which not only rendered them impervious to damp, but also gave the surface an added luminosity, to achieve 'the brilliancy of oil-painting, combined with the tender sweetness of water-colours'. The fixative was made of white wax dissolved in Spirits of Lavender. It was brushed onto the drawing and rubbed in with the fingers, then allowed to dry for twenty-four hours. Another coat could be applied if more transparency were required. When dry, the whole surface was rubbed with a clean nail or clothes brush to the required gloss. This fixative was not to be used over body colour. Haag gave the recipe to Winsor and Newton and was prepared for any other artist to try it.[5]

Notes

INTRODUCTION

1　RA Y 200/11-12/9 September 1842. Queen Victoria to Baron
 Stockmar
2　RA Add T 275
3　RA Z 491/22
4　RA Add C 4/213/5 August 1852. Marianne Skerrett was
 appointed Head Dresser to the Queen early in her reign. A
 plain little person, looking like 'Mrs Noah in a children's
 ark', Miss Skerrett was under five foot in height and 'thin as a
 shred of paper'. She was cultivated, intelligent, an excellent
 linguist and deeply religious. She fulfilled a far more
 important role in the Queen's life than her official title would
 suggest. For twenty-five years she was her confidante in many
 matters, carrying out endless useful tasks for her; organising
 many of the royal purchases of pictures and works of art,
 making practical arrangements with artists on the Queen's
 behalf and even biting the royal etching plates. Miss Skerrett
 was devoted to Landseer and many letters in her scarcely
 legible handwriting vouch for her efforts to smooth
 difficulties and persuade him to complete commissions on
 time.
5　RA Ponsonby letters, 17 November 1871
6　Ibid, 21 December 1872. Re: Henry Graves
7　Journal, 15 July 1846
8　Vivien Noakes, *Edward Lear* (1968), p74
9　Journal, 30 September 1846. For a discussion of Queen
 Victoria's own watercolours, see Marina Warner, *Queen
 Victoria's Sketchbook* (1979).
10　Ibid, 9 December 1846
11　RA Z 261/227v and 225v
12　RA Ponsonby letters, 24 May 1872. Henry Ponsonby served
 in the Grenadier Guards during the Crimean War, then
 became Equerry to Prince Albert and later the Queen. He
 was her Private Secretary from 1870 and Keeper of the Privy
 Purse from 1878. A wise counsellor, he wrote amusing and
 intelligent letters to his wife every day they were apart. See
 A. Ponsonby, *Henry Ponsonby* (1942)
13　Journal, 1 November 1836. The *Illustrated London News* (3
 September 1842) asserted that on her visit to Scotland in
 1842 the Queen expressed a wish to visit all the scenes of Sir
 Walter Scott's novels.
14　Ivor Brown, *Balmoral* (1955), p30. The book was partly
 written to refute this accusation, made in an essay by George
 Scott-Moncrieff.
15　Lord Cockburn, *Circuit Journeys* (1888; 1983 edition), p51.
 Just such a reading party takes place in A.H. Clough's *The
 Bothie* (1848), which opens with a description of Highland
 Games. The Queen quoted from this poem in the *Leaves from
 the Journal of Our Life in the Highlands*.
16　Ibid, pp195 and 220. Thomas Cook took his first excursion
 tour to Glasgow from Leicester in 1846, using the railways
 and the Scottish Steamer service (John Pudney, *Thos Cook &
 Son* (1978)).

17　Charles Dickens, *All the Year Round*, 15 February 1868, p240.
 For much information on the opening up of the Highlands,
 see James Holloway and Lindsay Errington, *The Discovery of
 Scotland* (National Gallery of Scotland, 1978).

CHAPTER ONE: THE FIRST VISITS TO SCOTLAND

1　Journal, 7 August 1842
2　Ibid, 12 September 1873
3　RA Y 90/56/8 September 1842. Queen Victoria to Leopold,
 King of the Belgians
4　The 5th Duke of Buccleuch was Lord Lieutenant of the
 County of Midlothian and Gold Stick of Scotland. His
 Duchess was Mistress of the Robes from 1841 to 1846.
5　RA Add U 171/151/11 September 1842. Queen Victoria to
 Princess Feodora of Hohenlohe-Langenburg
6　George IV had stayed at Dalkeith twenty years previously,
 when the Duke was a boy of fifteen.
7　Journal, 7 September 1842
8　*The Scotsman*, 10 September 1842
9　Journal, 8 September 1842
10　RA Z 287/13/11 September 1842. Queen Victoria to the
 Duchess of Kent. The previous year the Queen had employed
 six pipers at Windsor to play beneath the windows of rooms
 occupied by Prince Leopold, son of the King of the Belgians,
 'for his amusement' (RA Y 198/127/20 July 1841).
11　The Duke gave the Queen his portrait, painted by David
 Wilkie, wearing Highland dress. One of the rooms at
 Kensington Palace was furnished with Inverness tartan. After
 a luncheon given there in honour of the King of Prussia,
 Baron Bunsen described 'the Duke's colossal Highlander
 adding originality, if not charm, to the whole, by
 perambulating the dinner-table at the close with his
 deafening bagpipe – the more bewildering in its effects from
 the smallness of the space between the backs of the guests
 and the wall, the dining-chamber being small for the number
 of the party' (Frances, Baroness Bunsen, *Memoirs of Baron
 Bunsen* (1868), vol II, p9).
12　RA Y 90/56/8 September 1842. Queen Victoria to Leopold,
 King of the Belgians
13　RA M 35/18/18 September 1842. Prince Albert to Caroline,
 Dowager Duchess of Saxe-Gotha-Altenburg
14　Georgiana, Baroness Bloomfield, *Reminiscences of Court and
 Diplomatic Life* (1883), vol I, p48. Georgiana Liddell to
 Matilda Paget
15　RA S 14/25/10 March 1888. Louisa, 6th Duchess of
 Buccleuch to Queen Victoria
16　Mrs Oliphant, *Blackwood's Magazine*, February 1868, p4
17　The 6th Duke and Duchess spelt their name Athole; all
 others spelt it Atholl.
18　Journal, 12 September 1844
19　Much material in this chapter and in Chapter Two is taken
 from Lady Canning's letters and diaries, quoted by kind

permission of the Earl of Harewood. As it is not calendared, specific references are not given. Virginia Surtees, *Charlotte Canning* (1975), gives a detailed biography and account of Lady Canning's periods in Waiting on the Queen.

20 Journal, 16 September 1844
21 *Punch*, August 1844, p152
22 Journal, 21 September 1844
23 Ibid, 15 January 1843
24 Letters from Edwin Landseer to Jacob Bell are here quoted by kind permission of the Royal Institution.
25 Photography was still in its infancy in 1844, but one of the Athole officers, the Master of Strathallan, was 'busy with his calotype', attempting with varying success to take views and groups of those at the castle. As a final souvenir the Prince gave the Queen for Christmas 1845 a Highland Inkstand, which he had designed himself. It was made from granite, cairngorms and teeth from deer he had shot, surmounted by a roaring stag in frosted silver. On the panels round the sides were reproduced some of the watercolours painted by Lady Canning and Charles Landseer.
26 RA Y 91/61/28 September 1844. Queen Victoria to Leopold, King of the Belgians
27 RA Y 192/13/27 August 1847
28 Journal, 22 August 1847
29 RA Y 93/7/7 September 1847
30 RA Z 193/31/11 September 1847. Queen Victoria to the Prince of Leiningen
31 RA Z 193/32/20 September 1847. Queen Victoria to the Prince of Leiningen
32 Lord Frederick Hamilton in his memoirs (*The Days before Yesterday* (1920), p28) describes Landseer's wallpaintings and the royal visit to Ardverikie, as well as his brothers' annoyance at the banishment of the family to a nearby farm. As the house was destroyed by fire in October 1873, only one set of photographs and the Queen's own pencil copies record the appearance of the wallpaintings.
33 RA Z 171/25/4 September 1847. Queen Victoria to George Anson
34 RA Add C 4/19/10 November 1847. Marianne Skerrett to Edwin Landseer
35 RA Add C 4/20/20 December 1847. Marianne Skerrett to Edwin Landseer

CHAPTER TWO: THE FIRST YEARS AT BALMORAL

1 Lord Cockburn, *Circuit Journeys* (1888; 1983 edition), p87
2 *Two Generations*, ed Osbert Sitwell (1940), pp87-104
3 RA PP Balmoral 224/2 February 1848
4 Sir James Clark, the royal physician, considered that 'the dry bracing character of the atmosphere is just what the constitution of the whole Royal Family require, and if they could have the advantage of two months residence at Balmoral every year, it would be the means of improving the tone of their constitutions, mental as well as physical' (RA Y 206).
5 RA PP Balmoral 224/18 January nd
6 RA PP Balmoral 3/19 February 1848. On the death of Dr Robertson in 1881, the Queen wrote: 'He was clever & agreeable & much devoted to my beloved one, & dear

Mama, & was connected with the beginning of everything at Balmoral, the building of the new Castle, & the creation of the place, as it now is' (Journal).
7 Ibid, 5/May 1848
8 Ibid, 4/6 June 1848
9 Patricia Lindsay, *Recollections of a Royal Parish* (1904), p30
10 RA Y 93/48/13 September 1848
11 RA Y 93/49/20 September 1848
12 Journal, 10 September 1848
13 The material from the diaries and account books of James Giles in this chapter and Chapter Three is quoted by kind permission of his granddaughter Miss Mary Herdman.
14 Journal, 26 September 1848
15 RA Y 93/50/28 September 1848. Queen Victoria to Leopold, King of the Belgians
16 Journal, 28 September 1848
17 RA Add U 171/174/12 September 1849
18 RA Y 94/40/21 August 1849. Queen Victoria to Leopold, King of the Belgians
19 *Greville Memoirs*, ed L. Strachey and R. Fulford (1938), vol VI, pp185-86
20 RA Z 171/48/30 May 1849. Queen Victoria to George Anson
21 *Illustrated London News*, Supplement, 7 September 1850, pp216-17
22 RA Add A 24/289/27 September 1850. Queen Victoria to Harriet, Duchess of Sutherland
23 *Leaves* (Private edition, 1865), p13. The 'trim little boat' had just been built by Messrs Hall of Aberdeen.
24 Journal, 16 September 1850
25 Ibid, 17 September 1850
26 Ibid, 19 September 1850
27 Sir Charles Phipps was Treasurer and Private Secretary to Prince Albert; and Keeper of the Privy Purse from 1849 to 1866.
28 J.A.Manson, *Sir Edwin Landseer* (1902), p106
29 *The Athenaeum*, 6 May 1854
30 G.D. Leslie, *Riverside Letters* (1896), p199
31 G.D. Leslie, *The Inner Life of the Royal Academy* (1914), p163
32 RA Add C 4/363/19 November nd. Marianne Skerrett to Sir Edwin Landseer. The oil sketch is in the Royal Collection. For an up-to-date biography of Landseer, see Richard Ormond, *Sir Edwin Landseer* (1982).
33 RA PP Vic 21545/7 April 1851
34 RA Add J 1575/25 September 1852. William Wyld to a correspondent named Suzan. Lady Canning also thought the holiday in 1852 one of the most enjoyable. The Queen was 'fonder than ever of the place', the Prince's shooting was improving ('his "Gibier" not his skill') and the children were 'as merry as grigs'. She heard the Prince of Wales and Prince Alfred, who lived below her, 'singing away, out of lesson time as loud as ever can be'.

CHAPTER THREE: ARCHITECTURE AND INTERIORS AT BALMORAL

1 Journal, 22 September 1848. See Ronald Clark, *Balmoral* (1981), especially for the early photographs that complement the watercolours reproduced here.
2 RA PP Balmoral 83/10 November 1851
3 Ibid, 117/6 May 1852. In December 1852 Thomas Cubitt was

commissioned by the Prince to design a complete hot-water system for the new castle.

4 Ibid, 128/22 September 1852
5 Ibid, 130/19 October 1852
6 Ibid, 218/26 December 1856
7 Giles's watercolours were exhibited at the Architectural Institute of Scotland in Glasgow at Christmas 1854.
8 Journal, 6 and 7 September 1853
9 RA Y 149/68/12 September 1853
10 Twenty Years at Court, ed Mrs Steuart Erskine (1916), p268
11 See Roger Taylor, George Washington Wilson (1981) for material about this photographer's work for the Queen.
12 Leaves (Private edition, 1865), p54, 30 August 1856
13 RA Z 141/3/4 September 1856. New stables were completed by the summer of 1857 and a room where artists could stay was included next to the stable dormitory.
14 Leaves, 13 October 1856
15 Illustrated London News, 22 November 1851
16 Letters of Lady Augusta Stanley, ed Dean of Windsor and H. Bolitho (1927), pp102, 104. Lady Augusta was Lady in Waiting to the Duchess of Kent from 1846 to 1861, when she became Woman of the Bedchamber to the Queen. She married Arthur Stanley, Dean of Westminster, in 1863.
17 Memoirs of an Ex Minister (1884), vol I, p345, 1 September 1852
18 Journal, 22 August 1849
19 RA Z 193/50/20 November 1849
20 Leaves (Private edition, 1865), p49
21 Dearest Child, p143, 13 November 1858
22 RA PP Balmoral 191/1855 and 235/11 July 1857
23 Letters of Lady Augusta Stanley, op cit, p 72
24 Leaves (Private edition, 1865), p48. There had been doubt as to whether the newly plastered walls would be dry enough to be papered before the Queen and Prince arrived. They may have been merely tinted instead (RA PP Balmoral 200/23 July 1855).
25 Sir F. Ponsonby, Recollections of Three Reigns (1951), p15
26 RA Add U 291/8/p13. Copyright Heinrich C. Weltzien, Bonn, West Germany, 1985. Translated by Mrs de Bellaigue. Later in the century, one of the Queen's granddaughters was to find the same decoration rather less sympathetic. She described the effect of the carpets, chairs and curtains, all striped with greys, reds and black, as 'more patriotic than artistic', with a 'way of flickering before your eyes and confusing your brain' (Marie, Queen of Roumania, The Story of My Life (1934), p68).
27 RA Z 141/3/4 September 1856. Prince Albert to the Prince of Wales
28 Life and Letters of George, 4th Earl of Clarendon, ed Sir Herbert Maxwell (1913), vol II, p128, 30 August 1856
29 Ibid, p148, 31 August 1857
30 Ibid, p151, 11 September 1857. Count Lavradio arrived on 9 September for two nights.
31 A. Ponsonby, Henry Ponsonby (1942), p116
32 RA Add A 8/1832/22 October 1868

CHAPTER FOUR: THE QUEEN'S INTEREST IN TARTAN AND THE HIGHLAND GAMES

1 In June 1789, the royal Princes attended a masquerade in Hammersmith, 'all dressed alike as Highland Cheifs; nothing could be more Ellegant or becoming than their dress'. The Prince of Wales had just received a bill for £50.15s from Richard Farquhar for making his costume, with a 'Belted Kilt & Plaid Coat & Waistcoat of Silk with rich imbroidered Buttons & Thesels', an embroidered Scotch bonnet and two pairs of silk hose (Betsy Sheridan's Journal, ed William Le Fanu (1960), 14 June 1789; and RA Georgian Papers 29234/12 June 1789).
2 For a recent survey of the subject, see Hugh Trevor-Roper, The Invention of Tradition (1983).
3 T.B. Macaulay, History of England (1848; Everyman edition, 1953), vol II, p617
4 RA LPC 8/7 December 1834
5 RA LPC 37/13 January 1837. Princess Victoria to Louise, Queen of the Belgians
6 RA Y 10/35/28 November 1842. Louise, Queen of the Belgians, to Queen Victoria
7 When the Queen returned to the south from Blair Castle, The Times noted (9 October 1844) that Mr Macdougall of the Tartan Warehouse at Inverness had just received an order from her for a supply of very fine tartan of Duke of Rothesay pattern for the use of the Prince of Wales.
8 Journal, 26 August 1847
9 Ibid, 11 September 1848. Prince Leopold, although he was not taken to Balmoral until 1860, wore Highland dress from 1857.
10 After her husband's death, the Empress Frederick sent all his Highland dress back to the Queen at Balmoral (RA Z 42/26/4 August 1880). In December 1901 Edward VII returned it to the Kaiser, who said that it gave him great pleasure to recall standing in his father's dressing-room as a boy, admiring the 'precious and glittering contents of his box of Highland clothes'. He recollected the last occasion on which he himself had worn Highland dress, when visiting his grandmother at Balmoral in 1878.
11 RA T 5/1a/6 January 1867. Queen Victoria to the Prince of Wales
12 Journal, 2 October 1898. As Duke of Windsor, he was painted in a kilt by Sir James Gunn while exiled in Paris during the 1950s (National Portrait Gallery). Lady Donaldson refers to him dressing up in a kilt and playing the pipes to entertain his guests (Edward VIII (1974), p172).
13 Punch, 1844, p152
14 Journal, 14 September 1847
15 Ibid, 25 September 1848
16 Baron von Moltke, aide-de-camp to Prince Frederick William of Prussia on his visit to Balmoral in 1855, described walking to Abergeldie with the young Ladies in Waiting in their normal country wear of 'thick nailed boots, brown stockings, looped up short petticoats, and round hats, and with short sticks in their hands'. Lady Augusta Bruce ('rather stout') was unable to manoeuvre the walls, hedges and steep hills strewn with boulders (Moltke's Letters to his Wife (1896), vol I, p254, 30 September 1855).

17 Twenty-six years later, when the Queen visited Achnacarry, Sir Henry Ponsonby described in a letter to his wife how Lochiel appeared 'in his quiet kilt & plaid of Cameron tartan – quiet I mean as he wore it like a gentleman wears his every day suit, and was not girt about with gay buttons, dirks and nonsenses. Here was Locheil whose ancestor had done his best – and without him the rebellion of '45 would never have occurred – talking to The Queen whose ancestor he wished to turn out – and yet she liked him the better for it – and I a loyalist – or Hanoverian as some would say felt quite touched by the whole scene and for an instant almost a jacobite' (RA Ponsonby letters, 13 September 1873).

18 *Life and Letters of George, 4th Earl of Clarendon*, ed Sir Herbert Maxwell (1913), vol II, p151. Some Englishmen who rented estates in the Highlands became devoted to the costume of the north. Lord Cockburn mentions 'a respectable and middle-aged gentleman, who, though called Mackenzie, is, by birth, education and residence (till lately) a Middlesex Englishman', who wore 'full Celtic garb' because he had taken shooting in Nairn and 'pleased to fancy himself a Highlander' (*Circuit Journeys* (1888; 1983 edition), p163, 18 April 1845).

19 *Illustrated London News*, 30 September 1848

20 RA Add Q 2/26-8/24 September 1870

21 Information kindly supplied by Dr Micheil MacDonald

22 Journal, 28 September 1850

23 RA PP Balmoral 115, 137, 187, 272 and 376

24 Journal, 22 September 1848. The following year, Lady Augusta Bruce described the Queen and Prince at Balmoral 'armed with an immense Gaelic dictionary as large as themselves, which they studied the whole time' (*Letters of Lady Augusta Stanley*, ed Dean of Windsor and H. Bolitho (1927), p39).

25 RA PP Balmoral 95 and 134; RA Add Q 1/20 and 24

26 *Fraser's Magazine*, February 1868, p161

27 *Illustrated London News*, 4 September 1847

28 *Twenty Years at Court*, ed Mrs Steuart Erskine (1916), p170, 21 July 1848

29 *Leaves* (Private edition, 1865), p76

30 Journal, 9 September 1852 and 15 September 1853

31 RA L 18/123/27 August 1874, Queen Victoria to Henry Ponsonby, and RA L 26/120/29 August 1874, Henry Ponsonby to Queen Victoria

32 RA Add Q 5/19 and 82

CHAPTER FIVE: 'THIS DEAR PARADISE'

1 RA Z 194/21/8 September 1853

2 Much material in this chapter and in Chapter Six is taken from the diaries of Carl Haag, by kind permission of his granddaughter Mrs Allison.

3 RA Z 194/39/nd

4 In Waiting at Balmoral the following autumn, Eleanor Stanley commented gloomily that when the Prince missed his prey it 'did not signify as far as use went, but only for the honour and glory', as they had eaten a haunch of venison every day. She imagined that they would continue to do so for the rest of the visit, as there were already another twenty-two in the larder (*Twenty Years at Court*, ed Mrs Steuart Erskine (1916), p272).

5 Journal, 6 September 1850. When the Queen and Prince went up the mountain for the first time in 1848, the ascent took four hours. In 1873 Henry Ponsonby climbed and descended the mountain in that time, 'so it is nothing very big'. He was annoyed when someone told the Queen, as she 'does not like its being considered an easy thing to be done in an afternoon' (RA Ponsonby letters, 13 October 1873).

6 Ibid, 30 September 1853

7 RA Add U 171/205/18 October 1853. Lord Byron's poem 'Lachin y Gair' was first published in *Hours of Idleness* (1807).

8 *The Daily News*, 6 October 1853

9 *The Times*, 6 October 1853. That autumn was a difficult one for the Queen and Prince. He wrote to the Dowager Duchess of Coburg that they would have greatly enjoyed their stay in Scotland, 'were it not for the horrible Eastern complications' (RA M 42/79/27 September 1853). Before going north, the whole family, except the two youngest children, had had the measles; Prince Albert was particularly ill.

10 RA Z 289/9/5 October 1853. Queen Victoria to the Duchess of Kent

11 Journal, 10 October 1856

12 RA Add U 32/11 October 1859

13 The view of Kilchurn Castle was acquired at the exhibition of the Society of Painters in Watercolour. It was later among the paintings from the Royal Collection reproduced in the *Art Journal* and subsequently published in four volumes as *The Royal Gallery of Art* (nd).

14 Prince Albert complained to Baron Stockmar that, by 21 August 1860, 'we have not hitherto had one summer's day, and yet, according to the calendar the summer is nearly over! Here there is no living in the house without a fire, and if you go out, you get frightfully wet'. Nevertheless, on one day the Prince shot fifty grouse (RA Y 151/72). Artists were only supplied with ponies to ride with the Prince's express permission. The Queen said later that only Landseer, who stood 'in an exceptional position', was automatically allowed one.

15 RA PP 2/46/1204/8 November 1860. George Fripp to Sir Charles Phipps

16 RA Z 491/21

CHAPTER SIX: AFTER THE DEATH OF THE PRINCE

1 RA Z 261/250v

2 RA Z 261/249v/2 June 1862

3 *Dearest Mama*, p59, 2 May 1862

4 RA PP Balmoral 344/16 May 1862 and 342/3 May 1862

5 *All the Year Round*, p240, 15 February 1868

6 RA Z 261/250v

7 A. Macgeorge, *Wm. Leighton Leitch, A Memoir* (1884), pp63-64

8 RA Add U 143. Richard Leitch painted nine watercolours, for which he was paid £115.10s, with £30 for his travelling expenses. 'Lenchen' was the nickname for Princess Helena, Queen Victoria's third daughter.

9 *Wm. Leighton Leitch*, op cit, p64

10 Ibid, p 65, 6 October 1863. Jane, Baroness Churchill, was Lady of the Bedchamber from 1854.

11 *Dearest Mama*, p268, 17 September 1863

12 **Ibid**, p270, 22 September 1863
13 *Journal*, 20 October 1863
14 **The** Queen thought even Leitch's unfinished sketches 'valuable & His vy. slightest' lovely. She wanted to be able to give examples of his work to her children. For almost £100, about forty drawings and two albums of sketches were acquired on the Queen's behalf (RA L 20/9-11/12-13 March 1884).
15 *Journal*, 9 August 1864
16 Ibid, 7 December 1864
17 Plates 81-84 and colour plate XXI were among the illustrations in the private edition of the *Leaves*.
18 *Your Dear Letter*, p51, 23 December 1865
19 RA Add U 32/21 December 1867
20 RA Add A 32/5/1 October 1867. Queen Victoria to Arthur Helps
21 *Journal*, 17 January 1868
22 RA Add U 32/22 January 1868. Queen Victoria to the Crown Princess
23 *Your Dear Letter*, p165, 18 December 1867
24 *Pall Mall Gazette*, 10 January 1868
25 RA Add U 32/14 March 1868. Queen Victoria to the Crown Princess. The *Leaves* was translated into many languages, including Hindi. The Maharaja of Benares gave the Queen a special copy of this edition with a marble-work cover that he had designed and a hand-painted frontispiece, showing him presenting the book to the Queen.
26 RA Add A 32/11/11 December 1867. Queen Victoria to Alice Helps
27 RA Z 261/120/12 October 1859
28 RA Add U 143/28 May 1863
29 *Journal*, 4 June 1863
30 RA Add U 143/1 June 1863. Queen Victoria to Princess Alice
31 RA Add U 32/26 May 1864. Queen Victoria to the Crown Princess
32 RA Y 107/17/14 October 1861. Queen Victoria to Leopold, King of the Belgians
33 RA S 8/67/11 October 1861. Duchess of Athole to Queen Victoria
34 *Journal*, 9 October 1861
35 RA Add U 143/11 June 1865. Queen Victoria to Princess Alice
36 RA Y 166/60/10 June 1868. After these problems, Haag made all his patrons sign a form when he sold them a picture, by which the artist retained the copyright.
37 RA Add A 34/46/4 October 1889. Arthur Bigge to Sir Henry Ponsonby. Her Private Secretaries agreed that 'these Loan Exhibitions are becoming very voracious'.
38 *Journal*, 8 July 1899
39 *Mary Ponsonby, Memoirs and Letters*, ed Magdalen Ponsonby (1927), p59, 9 May 1865
40 *Journal*, 6 May 1865
41 RA Add U 292/23/3 April 1868. These were Queen Victoria's titles for the prints of *Sunshine* and *Shadow* that she sent Lord Derby.
42 RA PP Vic 279/May 1867. Sir Edwin Landseer to Sir Thomas Biddulph
43 James A. Manson, *Sir Edwin Landseer* (1902), p169, June 1867

44 *Your Dear Letter*, p138, 10 June 1867
45 *Journal*, 1 October 1873

CHAPTER SEVEN: THE LAST YEARS

1 *Leaves* (Private edition, 1865), p13
2 Ibid, p14
3 *Journal*, 18 August 1862
4 RA Add Q 1/56/29 January 1866. Queen Victoria to Dr Robertson
5 RA Add U 32/9 September 1867
6 *Journal*, 1 October 1868
7 RA Ponsonby letters, 9 November 1879
8 RA Y 165/82/13 September 1883. Queen Victoria to Sir Theodore Martin
9 For Simpson's visit to Abergeldie, see his *Autobiography*, ed G. Eyre-Todd (1903). Simpson describes the kindness of his host and the resulting difficulty in finding time to draw, as well as embarrassment over the inadequacy of his wardrobe. Some of Simpson's pictures were eventually reproduced in the *Illustrated London News* (12 September 1885). All the figures were altered from his original watercolours and no royal persons were portrayed.
10 C. Kingsley, *Fraser's Magazine*, February 1868, pp166-67
11 *Journal*, 5 October 1881
12 Ibid, 10 October 1881. In December 1883, Green was permitted to style himself 'Instructor of Landscape Painting in Watercolours in Ordinary to Her Majesty'.
13 Ibid, 4 June 1895
14 *Illustrated London News*, 6 May 1893
15 *Journal*, 4 October 1894
16 Professor Pagenstecher temporarily improved the Queen's cataracts with belladonna.
17 *Lady Lytton's Court Diary*, ed M. Lutyens (1961), p76. The Emperor's visit coincided with the date when the Queen had reigned longer than any other British sovereign.
18 RA PP Vic 16293/1896/11 January 1897
19 *Life with Queen Victoria: Marie Mallet's Letters from the Court 1887-1901*, ed V.Mallet (1968), see passim. Marie Adeane was a Maid of Honour from 1887 to 1891 and Extra Woman of the Bedchamber after her marriage.
20 RA Add A 30/297/5 August 1900. Queen Victoria to the Duchess of Albany
21 *Journal*, 7 September 1900
22 Ibid, 24 September 1900
23 Ibid, 6 November 1900

APPENDIX

1 *The Athenaeum*, 11 May 1850
2 Ibid, 30 April 1853
3 *Illustrated London News*, 14 May 1853, with illustration
4 RA K 42 f 13v
5 Aaron Penley, *The English School of Painting in Water Colours* (nd), p131

Index